GIFTS AND GRACES

GIFTS AND GRACES

A commentary on 1 Corinthians 12-14

by

Arnold Bittlinger

(Translation from German by Herbert Klassen and supervised
by the Rev Michael Harper)

WILLIAM B. EERDMANS PUBLISHING COMPANY
GRAND RAPIDS, MICHIGAN

English translation © 1967 by A. Bittlinger

First U.S. edition published by
William B. Eerdmans Publishing Company
July 1968
Library of Congress Catalog Card Number:
68-28848
ISBN 0-8028-1307-0
Printed in the United States of America

Reprinted, May 1976

ISBN 0-8028-1307-0

Foreword

The following Bible studies by Arnold Bittlinger were delivered at an ecumenical conference on "Charismatic Church Life". In preparation for printing they have been expanded somewhat and notes have been added. The lively lecture-style has been preserved as far as possible.

Questions concerning the Holy Spirit and His gifts have become a live issue in the ecumenical movement. The Commission on Faith and Order in all parts of the world is pursuing an intensive study of the relationship of the New Testament gifts to the renewal and unity of the church.

The following study is a useful contribution to this discussion. I pray that this book will get a wide hearing and help churches of all denominations and confessions to become the Spirit-filled Church of Jesus Christ.

Dr. WALTER J. HOLLENWEGER
Executive-Secretary of the Department
on studies in evangelism in the
World Council of Churches

The verses quoted in this
publication are from the
Revised Standard Version
of the Bible, copyrighted
1946 and 1952.

Preface

The renewed interest in, and experience of charismatic gifts in churches the world over, demand a careful study of these chapters in I Corinthians. But there is a further reason why this book is so important and useful. One of the chief handicaps, which has confronted commentators who have sought to deal adequately with these chapters in the past, is the lack of practical experience of these phenomena. In some sections they have been writing about purely hypothetical matters. However, the significance of this book lies in the fact that it is one of the first to be written, outside Pentecostal literature, by someone who has fairly wide experience of these manifestations in churches in West Germany. Even when scholarship is dedicated and inspired, it will obviously lack some quality if it is denied the experience of the very matters being dealt with.

This is not a subject for the dilettante. These gifts are capable of both constructive and destructive effects. They can unite and divide. But those who are serious about a truly biblical and catholic renewal of the Church cannot avoid the charismatic dimension.

Writing in the paper *Parish and People* (March 1966), Rev. John Sweet, Chaplain of Selwyn College, Cambridge, deals briefly with this subject under the heading "Spiritual breakthrough?" Referring to the charismatic renewal in the churches, prophesied by Lesslie Newbigin in his book *Household of God*, he says, "I am deeply impressed by what I have heard and read and think it should be welcomed (critically) by all concerned with renewal. But it could all be bedevilled by unsophisticated use of the New Testament—one side claiming too much, the other allowing too little. I Corinthians 12–14 is bound to be the main battle-ground."

So it is my responsibility in this preface to lead the reader onto the battle-ground. But it is my sincere desire and prayer that we shall speedily beat our swords into ploughshares, and recognize the fact that, although many skirmishes have been fought over these chapters in the past, the ground is really meant for sowing and reaping. So may we plough straight furrows through these chapters. Our ploughshares may well turn up some broken lances and other rusty relics of past warfare, but that does not alter the fact that this ground is meant for farming not fighting. And one sincerely hopes that this book will be a means of exorcising some of the devils of unsophisticated exegesis which John Sweet refers to in his article.

To one who was present when the lectures, from which this book is chiefly derived, were first delivered, it seemed an obvious task to get them translated and published in English. they were given as a series of Bible Studies at an Ecumenical Conference in 1965, held at Koenigstein, near Frankfurt in West Germany. It was at this Conference that I had a truly ecumenical experience, when I sat between an Orthodox Bishop and a German Baptist Minister, in a Roman Catholic Chapel, for a Pentecostal service conducted by an American Lutheran Pastor.

Finally, I should like to express my gratitude to Herbert Klassen for his translation of the original MS, and to Simon Barrington-Ward, the Dean of Magdalene College, Cambridge, for his careful reading of the MS, his many helpful suggestions, and his encouragement throughout.

MICHAEL HARPER

Contents

PART I

CHAPTER TWELVE

A Comparison of Christian and Pagan "Pneumatists"
(1 Cor 12:1-3)

"Now concerning spiritual gifts, brethren, I do not want you to be uninformed. You know that when you were heathen, you were led astray to dumb idols, however you may have been moved. Therefore I want you to understand that no one speaking by the Spirit of God ever says 'Jesus be cursed!' and no one can say 'Jesus is Lord' except by the Holy Spirit."

In verse 1 ("Now concerning spiritual gifts . . .") Paul is answering a question put to him by the Corinthians. In order to understand this properly we will have to have a close look at their correspondence.

Paul founded the church at Corinth on his second missionary journey (he remained at Corinth for one and a half years!). Sometime later Paul received news to the effect that members of the church had fallen back into sin—particularly immorality. Paul wrote a letter in response in which he warned them against associating with offenders.

This letter (we can call it Letter A) was lost. There is an allusion to this letter in 1 Corinthians 5:9, "I wrote to you in my letter not to associate with immoral men."

The Corinthians responded to this letter with Letter B. Apparently they misunderstood a few of the apostle's statements (see 2 Pet 3:15, 16). They also asked Paul a few new questions. This letter B is also lost; but we know the questions the Corinthians asked because he took them up in our so-called first letter to the Corinthians (Letter C), see e.g., 7:1,

Now "concerning the matters about which you wrote."

So in 1 Corinthians Paul is answering questions put to him by the church, e.g., questions about marriage, the resurrection of the dead, associating with pagans, a collection for Jerusalem, and also spiritual gifts.[1]

Paul does not consider these questions irrelevant; he gives exact answers: "I do not want you to be uninformed . . ." It belongs to the dignity and honesty of a Christian to use his mind in enquiring into questions affecting his faith and to seek clarity on them. Every Christian needs to be informed and to have a thorough knowledge of issues that confront him.[2]

In verse 3 Paul uses an expression ("I want you to understand") commonly employed in the official decrees of the Seleucid rulers. He is making use of an "official style" here. He is speaking with the authority of a Spirit-filled teacher, who announces officially: "It is so!" Not every Christian has the responsibility and right to lay down teaching—only the teacher commissioned and authorized by God (Eph 4:11; 1 Cor 12: 28, 29; Acts 13:1, etc). See James 3:1 "Let not many of you become teachers, my brethren, for you know that we who teach shall be judged with greater strictness."

A great deal of trouble is caused by people who appear on the scene as teachers, without ever having been commissioned by God. The church *must* be taught—but only by people whom God has specially called and to whom He has given the gift of teaching (Rom 12:7) as well as the gift of knowledge (1 Cor. 12: 8).

In verse 2 ("when you were heathen") Paul glances back at the pagan past of the Corinthians. For Paul there is a clear *once* and *now* in the life of a Christian: "*Once* you were darkness, but *now* you are light in the Lord!" (Eph 5:8). This "once" and "now" represents a clear break in the life of a Christian that others also notice: "For they themselves report . . . how you turned to God from idols" (1 Thess 1:9).

For "idols" Paul uses the diminutive form "little idols" in the text, alluding possibly to the many little bronze statues[3] which were to be found in every pagan home. In Jewish polemic these "little gods" were often designated as "dumb".

For example, in Habakkuk 2:18,19: "What profit is an idol when its maker has shaped it, a metal image, a teacher of lies? For the workman trusts in his own creation when he makes dumb idols! Woe to him who says to a wooden thing, 'Awake'; to a dumb stone, 'Arise'! Can this give revelation? Behold, it is overlaid with gold and silver, and there is no breath at all in it."

In sharp and ironic contrast to this absurdity he states: "You were led astray to dumb idols, however you may have been moved." This is probably an allusion to the practice of pagan ecstatic cults where the initiate was seized and violated by demonic power.[4] The point of comparison is clear. These little gods could not give them any clear direction or help—they were dumb—but the demonic powers behind them were violating and destroying their lives.

In contrast to this the Holy Spirit "speaks" and "helps". He never violates an individual, never attacks and destroys him, but rather brings the actual gifts and potentialities of a person to full development.

We only become real people when the Holy Spirit takes up residence in us. The comparison of pagan and Christian "pneumatists" makes it clear that the *pagan* is controlled by ridiculous dumb idols that do violence to him; the *Christian* is led by an exalted God who speaks and who liberates the individual to become his true self. In verse 3 Paul compares the "pneumatist" with the false teacher. The question the Corinthians asked was probably: "In a meeting for worship can

15

someone inspired by the Spirit of God say 'Jesus be cursed'?" Apparently there were people in Corinth who said "Jesus be cursed" during public worship.[5]

There are commentators who think this has to do with Christians in a state of ecstasy. These exegetes maintain that Christians, in a similar way to pagans, became intoxicated to the point where they no longer knew what they were saying. Under these circumstances they even cursed Jesus.

This interpretation would seem to be wrong. Representatives of this view have clearly had no direct experience of Christian "ecstasy", for there are no legitimate grounds for making analogies between pagan (i.e., spiritist) and Christian phenomena.

In his comparison with paganism the point Paul is making is that a Christian *cannot* be violated in this way. The Spirit of God, as we encounter Him in the New Testament, violates no one; He only works in a Christian to the extent that the Christian makes room for Him.

A variation on this interpretation is that *unbelievers* are under consideration here. According to 1 Corinthians 14:23 there were cases of their attendance at meetings for worship. During the meetings these unbelievers became ecstatic and shouted: "Jesus be cursed!"

But it is well-nigh inconceivable to think that unbelievers cursed Jesus during a meeting for worship and that the Corinthians then asked Paul whether this was a Christian utterance.

W. Schmithals[6] says concerning this: "It is just as unlikely that a modern congregation whose minister blasphemed and cursed Christ from the pulpit, should enquire of the Synod whether this was a proper manner of Christian address, as that hearers in those days should think it possible that cursing Jesus (albeit in a state of ecstasy) was done in the name of God."

A third interpretation says that the people under consideration are *backslidden Christians*, half converted ones, who had turned their backs on Christianity—possibly because they did not want to face the practical consequences of the faith in their own lives. These are the ones that then said (without ecstasy) "Your Jesus be cursed!" There is a parallel to this in a letter of Ptolemy's, where backslidden followers of the Serapis cult cry "cursed be all the gods!". But here also it is inconceivable that any one should think that these expressions of backsliders were uttered "by the Spirit of God".

A further interpretation says it is not Christians who are saying "Jesus be cursed" but *Jews*. This theory has a number of points in its favour. The expression "anathema" is a Jewish term of excommunication, applied to everything unholy and unclean. And if we consider also that according to Deuteronomy 21:23 someone hanged ("crucified") was considered cursed of God, then it is fairly certain that unbelieving Jews (on the basis of the Torah) often said "Jesus is cursed".

But it is a *Christian* meeting for worship and the Christian church which is under consideration here. It is highly unlikely that there were any Jews there who could freely speak against Jesus, and above all there was no one there who imagined that such an expression was inspired by the Spirit of God. So we should reject this fourth interpretation as well.

Who then are the people saying "Jesus be cursed" in a Christian meeting for worship, while other Christians there assume that they are speaking as if they have been moved by the Holy Spirit? It must be people who do not regard the expressions "Jesus be cursed" and "Christ is Lord" as contradictory; in other words, people who separate the historic Jesus from the pneumatic Christ. There were people like this according to 1 John 2:22. These "Christians" said: "Jesus is not the Christ!" They bore witness to Christ, but not as the Jesus of Nazareth who "became flesh". John calls such people anti-Christian (1 John 4:2,3).

We encounter this same false teaching later in the Ophites, a gnostic sect which would not admit anyone to their fellowship who had not previously cursed Jesus. Origen reports on this in his book against Celsus.[7]

So there were people inside the Christian fellowship— Schmitthals makes a good case for the fact that they were the people of the so-called "Christ" party—who cursed the human Jesus in the meeting for worship, believing that they were speaking by the Spirit of God, the Spirit of the exalted Christ.

Paul is directing himself against this teaching when he says: "No one speaking by the Spirit of God ever says: 'Jesus be cursed!'" The oldest Christian confession "Kyrios Jesous"— "Jesus is Lord!" directly contradicts this cursing of Jesus.

To what extent could such a confession be made by the Holy Spirit alone? This confession was more than a formula that anyone could utter at will. It involved consequences: turning from idols and turning to God (v 2). It was not common *then* to recite confessions thoughtlessly. Throughout the early Church the confession of faith could not be spoken in the presence of unbelievers. Non-Christians (including baptismal candidates) were asked to leave the meeting for worship and the doors were locked behind them before the church confessed its faith.[8]

A confession of faith is at the same time a prayer. Whoever says "Jesus is Lord" is saying simultaneously "Jesus, *my* Lord!" A true confession of faith includes in it a commitment to Jesus. This commitment to Jesus is the foundation for what Paul goes on to say about spiritual gifts.

Spiritual gifts can only be exercised in the right way when they are an expression of a life-union with Jesus. This personal relationship to Jesus, which takes on form in the confession "Jesus is Lord", can only be brought about by the Holy Spirit.

2

The Nature of Spiritual Gifts
(1 Cor 12 : 4-6)

"Now there are varieties of gifts, but the same Spirit; and there are
varieties of service, but the same Lord; and there are varieties of
working, but it is the same God who inspires them all in every one."

In verses 4 to 6 the gifts of the Spirit are described in three ways
as *charismata, diakoniai,* and *energemata,* i.e., as gifts, ministries,
and workings. In his use of these three terms Paul is expressing
something about: the origin of the gifts; the way in which they
are experienced in the church; the purpose of the gifts.[1]

(a) The term *charismata* denotes the source of the gifts i.e.
divine *charis* (grace) becoming concrete.[2] God's *charis* is the
origin of every *charisma.* Literally *charisma* means "present"
(i.e. in every-day Greek a birthday present). The ascended
Christ has given presents to His Body: "When he ascended on
high he led a host of captives, and he gave *gifts* to men,"
(Eph 4:8). The origin of a *charisma* never lies in the person,
but in God's grace which surrounds him. It is essential to
bear in mind this origin whenever the gift is considered or
experienced.

(b) The term *diakoniai* i.e., ministries or services, points to
the way in which the gifts become real in practice. I do not
believe that *diakonia* is derived from *dia* and *konia* "through the
dust" (according to this folk-etymology *diakonia* means a
special humiliation and lowering) but from *dia* and *enkoneo,*

which means "to be in haste". *Diakonia* therefore means "eager readiness to serve".

In exercising a *charisma*, therefore, it is not a matter of lowliness or humiliation, but of willing action. It is not a matter of waiting until something "comes over me" and forces me, but a readiness to give out what God has placed in me—in the spirit of 2 Timothy 1:6, "Rekindle the gift of God that is within you."

(c) The gifts bring about definite effects. They are *energemata* i.e., outworkings. When a Christian exercises a *charisma* he is acting as a member of the Body of Christ, i.e., Jesus Himself is doing something through that person. Whatever Jesus does always brings concrete results. The goal of all gifts consists in the fact that something actually happens, that a person is helped, that the church is strengthened. And behind this whole activity stands the triune God who works "all in all" (1 Cor 15:28)—the God who encounters us as *pneuma*—Spirit, as *kyrios*—Lord, and as *theos*—God.

Over against this strong emphasis on unity—the *same* Spirit, the *same* Lord, the *same* God—stands the equally strong emphasis on variety—there are *varieties* of gifts[3], *varieties* of service, *varieties* of working. Paul uses a very strong Greek word here, *di-haireo*, which means to tear asunder, to split, to dismember. The nature of God is infinite variety. God is not uniform; He is always many-sided. This is apparent everywhere in the structure of the universe, and also for example, in the plurality of biblical writings with their variety of viewpoints—that defy restriction to any one special system of thought. This also applies to the spiritual gifts. The gifts of divine grace are clearly distinguished from one another; an eye is not an ear, nor is a hand a foot (cf. 1 Cor 12:15f). But the variety of God manifest in the gifts is limited, for its source, outworking, and purpose are channelled by the one Spirit—as we have just seen. "All these are inspired by one and the same Spirit, who apportions to each one individually as he wills" (1 Cor 12:11).

3

The Spirit becoming Visible
(*1 Cor 12 : 7*)

"To each is given a manifestation of the Spirit for the common good."

In verse 7 Paul is talking about the process by which the Spirit becomes manifest, i.e., visible. The Holy Spirit can only become visible where He is present. According to New Testament thought there are two kinds of people, those who have the Holy Spirit and those who do not (cf. 1 Cor 2:14f where Paul distinguishes between the natural and the spiritual man). In Jude 19 the worldly people are defined as "devoid of the Spirit". The following diagram will help to make the meaning clear:

The natural man is made up only of body, soul and a "God-shaped blank" (R. Otto)

| SOUL |
| BODY |

The natural (not born again) man, as a rule, experiences this emptiness as an indefinable longing, in the sense of Augustine's words: "O God, our hearts are restless within us until they find their rest in thee." This God-shaped blank (which we could also call the "human spirit", cf Rom 8:16) can only be filled by the Spirit of God, i.e., by God Himself. Any attempt at satisfaction through substitutes leaves a person restless and without peace, as the familiar hymn says, "from the best bliss that earth imparts, we turn unfilled to thee again." It is not until a person is born again of the Spirit of God that he finds peace and rest.

What happens at the new birth? The Spirit of God takes up residence in a person and fills the vacuum. The "natural" man becomes a "spiritual" man, and consequently a "complete" man.

The man not born again: The born again Christian:

SOUL	
BODY	

SPIRIT
SOUL
BODY

Every born again Christian has the Holy Spirit (John 3:5,6; Rom 8:9, 15, 16; Eph 1:13,14; 2 Cor 1:22; 5:5 etc.). The born-again-Christian "has" the manifestation of the Holy Spirit, but never in a static sense; rather as a dynamic process of "being taken possession of".

The Greek word *didotai* ("is given") denotes a present continual tense, i.e. the manifestation of the Spirit is not just given once, but again and again. The believer is constantly filled anew with the Holy Spirit. (You can compare this to the universe; the elements of the atom are constantly being renewed. Matter does not exist as something that *is*, but as something that is *happening*.) From the human standpoint this means a constant opening of oneself anew to the working of the Spirit. But the Spirit is not just given in an "invisible way". He wants to manifest Himself visibly. (Again this can be compared to creation; the invisible power of God that renews the atoms, becomes concrete and visible in matter.) In every individual that is born again the Spirit wants to become visible. One way in which the Spirit becomes visible is in the gifts of divine grace. Imagine a person who possesses all essential organs and limbs but is unconscious, so that his five senses are not functioning; he can neither see, nor hear, nor smell, nor taste, nor feel. Such an individual is alive and certainly must be looked upon as a human being, but he is out of contact with his environment. The senses with which he can establish contact are not functioning. Just as the human body exercises certain functions through the five senses, in like manner the spiritual gifts of the believer are necessary in order that the body of Christ can exercise certain functions. It is a matter here of awakening those gifts that lie dormant in every born again Christian (2 Tim 1:6). And what purpose does this manifestation of the Spirit through the gifts serve? The gifts are given "for the common good". They never exist to build up the individual member, although they do that also, but they always exist for the building up of the whole body of Christ (1 Cor 14:26; Eph 4:11-16). The Greek expression *pros to sympheron*—"for the common good" (notice the contrast with verse 2 *pros ta eidola*—"to the little idols") means literally "to bring together". We are dealing here with a technical term taken from Stoic philosophy which has a similar meaning to the Greek word *kosmos*. We can say therefore, that in exercising spiritual gifts we are involved in the restoration (the bringing together again) of God's perfect work in creation. An activity can only be characterized as a spiritual gift when it assists in the restoration of creation, and contributes towards the healing of a sick world. But it will also be true that every such activity and contribution is a gift of the Spirit, even when the individual involved is unconscious of it (cf. Matt 25:27f where the "gifted "people do not know that they exercised the gift of *diakonia*—service).

To *each* one gifts are given. The possession of spiritual gifts is therefore in no sense a measure of Christian maturity. Spiritual gifts are received as presents from God by every Christian who will accept them in childlike faith. The sinner who comes before God in his helplessness with the words "God have mercy on me a sinner" receives, to begin with, the basic gift, the *charisma* of eternal life (Rom 6:23). You cannot earn any gift or obtain it by labouring for it; it is only received by him who comes before God in his helplessness and grasps hold of the grace of God in simple trust. God places His gifts into our unholy hands and takes the risk of our misusing them. It is, therefore, of greatest importance that everyone who reaches out for these gifts of divine grace, should, at the same time, observe carefully the help and instruction then offered to protect against misuse. Pride seems to be a special danger (Rom 12:3). Confession of sin, in which we repeatedly acknowledge our personal unworthiness before God and, if necessary, another person, is one of the special means of protection against pride. Confession and *charisma* belong together (James 5:15, 16). Suffering also protects us against pride; therefore suffering and *charisma* also belong together (2 Cor 12:7). As a protection against individualism, which is another great danger, we have been given the congregation and its offices (apostles, prophets, teachers, etc.) — see 1 Corinthians 12:28f and Ephesians 4:11.

4

Different Types of Spiritual Gifts
(1 Cor 12:8-11)

"To one is given through the Spirit the utterance of wisdom, and to another the utterance of knowledge according to the same Spirit, to another faith by the same Spirit, to another gifts of healing by the one Spirit, to another the working of miracles, to another prophecy, to another the ability to distinguish between spirits, to another various kinds of tongues, to another the interpretation of tongues. All these are inspired by one and the same Spirit, who apportions to each one individually as he wills."

There are a number of places in the New Testament where the gifts of divine grace are listed (e.g., Rom 12:5-8; 1 Cor 12:8-10; 1 Cor 14:26f; Eph 4:11). The great multiplicity of gifts makes it clear that the activity of Jesus extends to the whole range of human experience. The list of gifts in 1 Corinthians 12:8-10 is concerned especially with the controversial gifts, those that were often misused or misunderstood. Because of this we shall examine each one of them in turn in the light of scripture, answering the following questions:

    (i) What is the nature of each gift?

    (ii) How did the gift arise in the Old Testament? (We will not list all the occurrences, but as a rule examine one example more closely.)

    (iii) How did Jesus exercise the gift?

    (iv) How did His disciples and the New Testament church practise the gift?

It should be clearly understood that in the following analysis we are only concerned with the *biblical* evidence.

(a) *The Word of Wisdom*

(i) In a difficult or dangerous situation a word of wisdom may be given which resolves the difficulty or silences the opponent. It is not innate wisdom as a personal possession which is described here, but rather a word of wisdom given to someone in a specific situation.

(ii) In the Old Testament King Solomon prayed to God for the gift of wisdom and received it from God (1 Kings 3:16–28). A difficult situation arises: two women come before Solomon with babies, one dead and one alive. Each mother insists that the living child is her own. One of the women had taken her own child which had suffocated during the night, and exchanged it for the child of the other woman while she was asleep. Because no witness was present the deceit cannot be exposed. The word of wisdom: Solomon says, "Bring me a sword . . . divide the living child in two, and give half to one, and half to the other." The result: the woman whose son was alive says, out of love for her child, "Give her the living child, and by no means slay it." But the guilty woman said, "It shall be neither mine nor yours; divide it." The response of the women to the word of wisdom immediately made it clear who was the mother of the living child. It says further, "And all Israel heard of the judgment which the king had rendered; and they stood in awe of the king, because they perceived that the wisdom of God was in him, to render justice." The word of wisdom is not human wisdom, but divine wisdom. This divine wisdom is greater than any human wisdom (1 Kings 5:10f).

(iii) Already in Isaiah 11:2 it was prophesied that "the Spirit of wisdom" (LXX *pneuma sophias*) would rest upon the Messiah. In Luke 2:40 we read the following about Jesus, "And the child grew and became strong, filled with wisdom; and the favour of God was upon him." We will take one example from the life of Jesus that demonstrates this divine wisdom in action (Luke 20:20–26). There is a difficult situation: as so often, Jesus' opponents put a catch-question to him: "Is it lawful for us to give tribute to Caesar or not?" If Jesus says yes, he will be considered a friend of the Romans and the Jews will hate him; if he says no, then his enemies can report him to Rome for sedition. Word of wisdom: Jesus requests a denarius and asks them: "Whose likeness and inscription has it?" When his opponents answer "Caesar's", Jesus says: "Then render to Caesar the things that are Caesar's, and to God the things that are God's." Result: "And they were not able in the presence of the people to catch him by what he said; but marvelling at his answer they were silent" (cf. also Luke 13:17; 14:6; 20:40).

(iv) Jesus promises his followers: "For I will give you a mouth and wisdom, which none of your adversaries will be able to withstand or contradict" (Luke 21:15). The early Christians experienced this gift of a word of wisdom in their daily lives, in the church and in their homes (Acts 6:3; 2 Pet 3:15); but above all when they faced martyrdom. This becomes particularly clear in the case of Stephen. We read the following in Acts 6:10: The opponents of Stephen, "could not withstand the wisdom and the Spirit with which he spoke." The word of wisdom, in this case, had a fatal effect. In Acts 7:57f we read, "they . . . stopped their ears and rushed together upon him. Then they cast him out of the city and stoned him." In other words, the disciples of Jesus have no guarantee that in uttering a word of wisdom they will find recognition. In the last analysis however, the death of Stephen did contribute to the spread of the Kingdom of God. For as a result of his death the church scattered abroad (Acts 8:1) and also one of the leaders in this persecution of the church was won over—Saul of Tarsus. And it is this same Saul who later, as the apostle Paul, asks in prayer that this gift of wisdom might be made available to all Christians (Eph 1:17). This wisdom lies hidden in Christ (Col 2:3). Because Christians are members of the body of Christ, it must be true that in a normal congregation the wisdom of Christ will repeatedly become visible in a "word of wisdom" (1 Cor 12:8).

(b) *The Word of Knowledge*

(i) The word of knowledge consists of the old message spoken in the new situation in such a way that it still remains the old message.

(ii) In the world in which the Old Testament came into being, the sun, moon and stars were regarded as divinities or as divine powers to which men prayed and on which they felt dependent. The old message that "God is Lord over *all* His creation" was so spelt out against the background of this world picture, that the sun, moon and stars were alike shown plainly to be lights created by God to serve men. The world was stripped of any divinity of its own. In this negation the sovereignty of God finds unequivocal expression. Man is now enabled to exercise dominion over the world just because he has his commission from God to do so. (When water, for instance, is no longer a divine power of chaos but H_2O—then man can confidently analyse it under a microscope. Modern science owes its very existence to this stripping away of false divinity. It follows that if man seeks to exercise his commission to control the world in isolation from the Giver of that commission, nature will again be made into a threatening power of chaos—cf. Gen 6:5f).

(iii) In Matthew 7 Jesus' hearers witness to the fact that He taught as One who had full divine authority and not as the scribes, who were learned only in the letter of the scriptures. The teaching of Jesus, and thus the word of knowledge to which He gave utterance, was essentially a proclaiming of say, in the Sermon on the Mount, the Old Testament commandments in a new situation, done in such a way that their essential aim, the establishment of love between God and man, was authentically realized in this new situation. When in Matthew 19:8 Jesus differentiated between His own teaching and that of Moses, He made it apparent that there had been a time when the one eternal will of God could give rise to a quite different interpretation in practice, from that demanded in the new situation to which He now spoke.

(iv) Jesus, according to John 14:26 promised the disciples that the Spirit would "bring to your remembrance all that I have said to you." This explains the way in which, in this very Gospel of John itself, the Spirit so recalled Jesus' words to His disciples that those words could meet the situation of the readers in the hellenistic world of the end of the first century, and they could meet them with the same cutting edge of the word that Jesus spoke in His own life to the Jews of Palestine. Thus the old message was addressed to the new situation in such a form that it remained the old message. To repeat the exact words would have been to distort the original message. (Anyone who thinks today that he can argue as to whether the seven day creation story is to be taken literally or symbolically by referring to the problems of modern atomic physics, and anyone who thinks he can deal with today's moral problems in the exact words of the book of Leviticus, is missing the actual intention of the Bible altogether. In his very literalism he is not being true to the Bible, but is in fact distorting the biblical message.)

Jesus, through the Holy Spirit, gave His disciples the "word of knowledge" so that they might ever and again avoid this distortion and be enabled to speak the word of God with its unchanging sharpness into the contemporary situation.

(c) *The Gift of Faith*

(i) The gift of faith is not to be confused with "saving faith", the possession of every Christian; nor with faith as a fruit of the Spirit (Gal 5:22), which every Christian should manifest. Here we are concerned with "faith that moves mountains" (Matt 17:20; 1 Cor 13:2) which is given as a gift of divine grace to individuals at specific times. The Roman Catholic theologian Joseph Brosch writes: "The gift of faith is nothing less than *fides miraculosa*, the power of the Holy Spirit manifested in order to accomplish the will of God despite all natural resistance, and above all, the power to triumph over a world at enmity with God."[1] "A Christian who has received this gift of divine grace has a supernatural conviction that God will reveal his power, righteousness and mercy in a specific case."[2]

(ii) The heroes of faith listed in Hebrews 11 show us that this gift was given to men and women in the Old Testament in rich measure. We will select one incident as an example. In 1 Kings 18 the following events are described: Elijah commands the people of Israel and the Baal prophets to come to Mount Carmel to witness a divine judgment. The pagan prophets build an altar for Baal and Elijah one for the God of Israel. An ox is laid on each altar, and the true God is to prove his power by sending fire from heaven to consume the sacrifice on the altar. Elijah did not need much courage to ridicule the prophets of Baal who danced around their altar for hours in a state of ecstasy shouting "Baal, answer us!" But it took more than courage, it took the gift of faith, for Elijah, after ridiculing them, to have water poured over the altar to eliminate any natural possibility of combustion, and then to pray "Answer me, O Lord, answer me, that this people may know that thou, O Lord, art God." One need hardly add that his prayer was answered, for the answer is included in the gift of faith.

(iii) This gift is also evident in the ministry of Jesus; as in John 11:41,42 where Jesus confronted by an already decaying Lazarus, prays "Father, I thank thee that thou hast heard me. I know that thou hearest me always, but I have said this on account of the people standing by, that they may believe that thou didst send me." Then he cried, "Lazarus, come out!".

In the case of Jesus—just as with Elijah—it becomes clear that the gift of faith is given, above all, to strengthen the weak faith of the people. J. Brosch writes: "Faith as a gift is essentially a tremendous assurance, received only by divine grace; an assurance which draws the supernatural into the natural world. An immovable faith such as this is particularly suited to win the weak and to establish them."[3]

(iv) During His human life the gift of faith was given to some people to such a degree that even Jesus was amazed. It says, for example, in the story of the centurion of Capernaum, "Jesus marvelled, and said to those who followed him, 'Truly, I say to you, not even in Israel have I found such faith'" (Matt 8:10). And to the Caananite woman Jesus said, "O woman, great is your faith!" (Matt 15:28; cf. also Mark 2:5). Jesus said specifically in Matthew 17:20 and Matthew 21:21 that such faith can move mountains and achieve the impossible. In Acts 3:16 Peter says after the lame man was healed, "And his name, by faith in his name, has made this man strong whom you see and know; and the faith which is through Jesus has given the man this perfect health in the presence of you all." The most remarkable example is in Mark 11:22-24, "Have faith in God. Truly, I say to you, whoever says to this mountain, 'Be taken up and cast into the sea,' and does not doubt in his heart, but believes that what he says will come to pass, it will be done for him. Therefore I tell you,whatever you ask in prayer, believe that you receive it, and you will." Jesus says here in so many words that the one who receives this gift can return to the routine of daily life directly after his prayer, because, what he has asked has already become reality to him, even if he and others do not yet see it. It must be remembered especially with the gift of faith that it is given by God and cannot be demanded by anyone. Neither can anyone count on this gift to make up what is lacking in his "measure of faith" (Rom 12:6).

(d) *The Gifts of Healing*

(i) The gifts of healing are primarily concerned with the healing of physical illness, but beyond this with restoration to health of the whole man, body, soul and spirit.

(ii) In the Old Testament God reveals Himself as the one who heals man: "I am the Lord, your healer" (Ex 15:26). Not only Jews are healed, but also pagans, for example the general Naaman (2 Kings 5). But it is not true that all men are healed indiscriminately. God has His own history of dealings with every human being. In the case of King Azariah, God saw it was right to let his illness continue to the end of his life, even though it says of him in 2 Kings 15:3 "He did what was right in the eyes of the Lord." We read in Numbers 12:10-15 that Miriam, for disciplinary reasons was ill for a certain time and could not be healed until this time, fixed by God, had elapsed.[4] Job also had to bear his suffering until he had arrived at a true understanding of God and himself: "I know that thou canst do all things, and that no purpose of thine can be thwarted. 'Who is this that hides counsel without knowledge?' Therefore I have uttered what I did not understand, things too wonderful for me, which I did not know. 'Hear, and I will speak; I will question you, and you declare to me.' I had heard of thee by the hearing of the ear, but now my eye sees thee; therefore I despise myself, and repent in dust and ashes" (Job 42:2–6). Others though, are healed instantaneously; for example, King Hezekiah (2 Kings 20:1–7).

(iii) On the basis of Isaiah 35:5,6 and 61:1 it was expected of the Messiah that he would heal the sick.[5] "Then the eyes of the blind shall be opened, and the ears of the deaf unstopped; then shall the lame man leap like a hart, and the tongue of the dumb sing for joy" (Isa 35:5,6). "The Spirit of the Lord God is upon me, because the Lord has anointed me to bring good tidings to the afflicted; he has sent me to bind up the brokenhearted, to proclaim liberty to the captives, and the opening of the prison to those who are bound" (Isa 61:1). Jesus relates these Old Testament promises to himself when he says: "Today this scripture has been fulfilled in your hearing" (Luke 4:21). In Luke 7:22 he uses these promises to confirm his Messiahship, when confronted with the questionings of John the Baptist. There is no incident in Scripture where someone who came to Jesus remained sick. Jesus healed not only the people of God, but also pagans like the slave of the Roman centurion and the daughter of the Canaanite women. Everyone who places his trust in Jesus is healed.[6] In Jesus the Kingdom of God has dawned. Satan has been robbed of his power (Luke 10:18 "I saw Satan fall like lightning from heaven"). Everyone who is touched by Jesus receives full salvation in body, soul and spirit. It is true that in the healing in John 9:3 it is said that there was a certain purpose in the illness—up to that point anyway—to reveal the works of God; and in John 11:14f it says that the faith of the disciples needed to be awakened; and in Mark 8:23–25 it is reported that the healing did not occur immediately but in stages. But nowhere does it say that anyone who came into direct contact with Jesus had to remain ill—even for a time. Jesus healed *all* who put their trust in Him.

(iv) The healings the apostles experienced, however, are more similar to the Old Testament. As with Jesus, others who do not belong to God's people are healed, for example, the lame men in Acts 3:6 and Acts 14:8–10, or the father of Publius the governor of Malta. But among Christians there are some who are not healed, as for example, Paul himself: "And to keep me from being too elated by the abundance of revelations, a thorn was given me in the flesh, a messenger of Satan, to harass me, to keep me from being too elated. Three times I besought the Lord about this, that it should leave me; but he said to me, 'My grace is sufficient for you, for my power is made perfect in weakness.' I will all the more gladly boast of my weaknesses, that the power of Christ may rest upon me" (2 Cor 12:7–9).

In Colossians 1:24 Paul suggests that such suffering can serve a substitutionary function: "Now I rejoice in my suffering for your sake, and in my flesh I complete what is lacking in Christ's afflictions for the sake of his body, that is, the church." Besides this there are some who are temporarily sick, like Timothy (1 Tim 5:23) and Trophimus (2 Tim 4:20). Sudden healings are reported, for example, in Acts 5:15; 9:34; 19:12. In the church, the body of Christ, the healing power of Jesus becomes visible in the gifts of healing. In Mark 16:18 this is promised to those that believe in Jesus. In James 5:14,15 it says: "Is any among you sick? Let him call for the elders of the church, and let them pray over him, anointing him with oil in the name of the Lord; and the prayer of faith will save the sick man, and the Lord will raise him up . . ." In 1 Corinthians 12:9 the Greek suggests the plural: gifts of healings. Every healing is a special gift. In this way the spiritually gifted individual stands always in new dependence upon the divine Giver. He must constantly look to God for His gift. There is no formula or technique whereby he can lay hold of God's healing power.

Note 1.

In answer to the question concerning the origin of disease the Bible repeatedly refers to Satan; for example Luke 11:14 "Now he was casting out a demon that was dumb; when the demon had gone out, the dumb man spoke." In Luke 13:16 it says the following about the woman with the twisted spine: ". . . a daughter of Abraham whom Satan bound for eighteen years". In Job 2:5,6 we read: " 'But put forth thy hand now, and touch his bone and his flesh, and he will curse thee to thy face.' And the Lord said to Satan, 'Behold, he is in your power; only spare his life.' " In this last instance, however, it is immediately apparent that Satan does not have infinite power to destroy but that God has set limits to his activity.

Note 2.

A second question that inevitably arises concerning the gifts of healing, is the relationship between divine healing on the one hand and medicine on the other. In Sirach 38 it says: "Honour a physician with the honour due unto him for the uses ye may have of him: for the Lord hath created him. For of the most High cometh healing . . . The Lord hath created medicines out of the earth; and he that is wise will not abhor them . . . With such doth he heal (men,) and taketh away their pains. Of such doth the apothecary make a confection . . . My son, in thy sickness be not negligent: but pray unto the Lord, and he will make thee whole . . . Then give place to the physician, for the Lord hath created him: let him not go from thee, for thou hast need of him. There is a time when in their hands there is good success. For they shall also pray unto the Lord, that he would prosper that, which they give for ease and remedy to prolong life." The opinion of this inter-testamental writer is that it is obviously not a question of "either/or" but of "both/and". It is a mark of falling away from God if one relies solely on the doctor. King Asa is accused of this in 2 Chronicles 16:12: "Asa was diseased in his feet, and his disease became severe; yet even in his disease he did not seek the Lord, but sought help from physicians." In the New Testament medical facilities are not disregarded. Jesus himself sent the leper that was healed for examination to the priests, the health department of that day, and in Mark 7:32f and John 9:6 he made use of physical means to awaken in the sick person the faith to be healed.[7]

Paul recommends wine as medicine for Timothy's stomach complaint in 1 Timothy 5:23, and in James 5:14 anointing with oil is prescribed. Incidents in Mark 3:10, Luke 6:19 and Luke 8:44, where Jesus acknowledges that people are healed who touch his clothes, strike us as rather strange. Similar incidents are also recorded in the experience of the apostles. We read in Acts 5:15 ". . . so that they even carried out the sick into the streets, and laid them on beds and pallets, that as Peter came by at least his shadow might fall on some of them." And in Acts 19:11,12 we read: "And God did extraordinary miracles by the hands of Paul, so that handkerchiefs or aprons were carried away from his body to the sick, and diseases left them and the evil spirits came out of them."

Heinz Doebert writes the following about these miracle stories: "One should not interpret these strange healings through contact with the clothes or the person of Jesus too readily as some kind of primitive mechanistic magic. Rather it points to an underlying belief that physical contact is involved in a genuine personal encounter . . . The sick people know that Christ heals as the Son of the living God. His clothes and his shadow are a part of Himself. What *He* can do, His clothes and shadow as symbols of Himself, can also do. It is not the clothes and the shadow that heal, but the presence of Jesus Christ represented in His clothes and shadow. These healings arise from the bodily presence of Jesus and through the direct encounter of the sick person with Christ.[8] These healings are deeds of faith and have nothing to do with magic, at least not with primitive magic as we understand it today. Whoever maintains that elements of magic have penetrated into the Bible at these points, denies the fact that in His temptation Jesus resisted the whole realm of magic, and suggests that the people who gave us these accounts knew less about man than does our enlightened age. We are involved here in what one might call sacramental healings, healings through the bodily presence of Jesus Christ, whose clothes one can touch because He is in fact within reach, and whose shadow is passed across us because He is personally going by and has encountered us . . . For the church of the ascended Lord the Lord's Supper is the place of tangible encounter with its Lord. In, with, and under the bread and wine the Lord is bodily present, ready to be encountered."[9]

(e) *The Working of Miracles*

(i) In contrast to the preceding gift, the gift of working miracles touches not only on healing but covers a wide range of mighty deeds of every kind. These are suited to the varied situations which call forth the exercise of this gift.

(ii) In the Old Testament many mighty miracles are recorded: Elijah and Elisha, for example, raised the dead. In addition countless nature miracles occur: the plagues in Egypt; the crossing of the Red Sea; miracles during the desert wandering; and during the occupation of Canaan. The working of miracles often substantiated the prophetic word; for example in 1 Kings 13:1f where a prophet from Judah declared that worship at Bethel would cease, and this, just as King Jeroboam was sacrificing at the altar. In verses 4 to 6 it says: "And when the king heard the saying of the man of God, which he cried against the altar at Bethel, Jeroboam stretched out his hand from the altar, saying 'Lay hold of him.' And his hand, which he stretched out against him, dried up, so that he could not draw it back to himself . . . And the king said to the man of God, 'Entreat now the favour of the Lord your God, and pray for me, that my hand may be restored to me.' And the man of God entreated the Lord; and the king's hand was restored to him, and became as it was before." That the gift of miracles— like every gift—can be misused becomes strikingly clear in the life of Samson. This Old Testament judge used the gift given to him to fulfil his own personal desire for revenge. One supposes that Elisha in 2 Kings 2:23,24 was misusing his gift when he allowed forty-two children to be devoured by bears after they had ridiculed him.

(iii) In the life of Jesus the working of miracles covers a wide field. We read that He raised the dead, drove out demons, and also did nature miracles. Here as well, we shall take one example from many, Mark 4:35f. Jesus is on the Sea of Galilee with His disciples. He is sleeping in the back of the boat when a storm blows up and threatens to destroy the boat. Jesus is awakened by His frightened disciples and He rebukes the wind and says to the sea, "Peace! Be still". The wind ceased and a great stillness came over all. Great fear came over the disciples and they said to one another, "Who then is this, that even wind and sea obey him?" The gift of working miracles has something in common with the word of wisdom. As a rule, there is a dangerous situation, then the mighty deed happens, and the result is that the danger is averted. In the case of the word of wisdom, the danger is usually of a spiritual nature, and only indirectly is life endangered, whereas the situation that calls for the working of a miracle usually involves the physical and a direct threat to body and life.

(iv) In John 14:12 Jesus promised all believers, "Truly, truly, I say to you, he who believes in me will also do the works that I do; and greater works than these will he do, because I go to the Father." In the strength of this the church, when faced with a great danger, prayed, "And now, Lord, look upon their threats, and grant to thy servants to speak thy word with all boldness, while thou stretchest out thy hand to heal, and signs and wonders are performed through the name of thy holy servant Jesus" (Acts 4:29,30). Paul often preached the Gospel in a godless, antagonistic environment and yet he could write "my speech and my message were not in plausible words of wisdom, but in demonstration of the Spirit and power" (1 Cor, 2:4). And in Acts 19:11 we read, "And God did extraordinary miracles by the hands of Paul." The early apostles raised the dead (Acts 9:36–42; 20:7–12), cast out evil spirits (Acts 16:18; 19:12), and performed nature miracles (Acts 16:26; 28:3f). Joseph Brosch writes: "From every place to which messengers of Christ went, reports came back of how they had been granted the gift of miracles. It was in keeping with the promise Christ made when He gave the Great Commission, that one of the criteria in the expansion of the early church was that she should move forward in Spirit and power. If the tools God had chosen for the proclamation of the good news were lowly, then all the more could He accomplish mighty deeds with His tools and so make foolish the wisdom of the world".[10] The church as the body of Christ has a claim on the miracle-working power of Jesus. This power becomes visible in the gift of working miracles. Paul writes to the Galatians about Christ as the one ". . . who supplies the Spirit to you and works miracles among you."

(f) *The Gift of Prophecy*

(i) Prophecy is not in the first instance, foretelling, but rather, forth telling — light for the present (which can, however, involve a glance back into the past or a look into the future).

(ii) The gift of prophecy is very common in the Old Testament. The revelation of God is received in various ways by the prophets. In the earliest period, visions seemed to play a special role, for according to 1 Samuel 9:9 prophets were originally called "seers". But in the classical prophets and in the post-exilic period, although the revelations of God were often received in visions, as for example Isaiah 6:1; Jeremiah 1:11,13; Ezekiel 1:4f; Zechariah 1:8, etc., the word of God was also received audibly. Already in the life of Samuel the Lord spoke to him during the night concerning the judgment on the house of Eli (1 Sam 3:9f). In Isaiah 6:8f in connection with his call, God had a discussion with Isaiah. Jeremiah's call in Jeremiah 1:4f represents a parallel incident. Finally, we also encounter the phenomenon whereby the prophet who is facing the people of

God, has a word of God put directly into his mouth (see Jer 1:9, "I have put my words in your mouth") and he declares the word of God spontaneously, without having had a previous vision or having heard the voice of God. 2 Chronicles 20:14f represents an example of this: in the midst of the people of God the Spirit of the Lord comes upon Jahaziel, and he prophesies. We meet this speaking under direct inspiration above all in prophetic dialogues and debates where the truth is being contested, as for example in Amos 7:16,17, where Amos is debating with the priest Amaziah. It is interesting to notice that God forces the non-Israelite Balaam to prophesy against his will (Num 23:5f). When called to task by his master he says, "Must I not take heed to speak what the Lord puts in my mouth?"

The Old Testament prophet does not speak on his own authority, but transmits what he has seen or heard from God, i.e., what God Himself has put in his mind and mouth. A parallel example that makes this relationship abundantly clear can be seen in Exodus 7:1,2 where God says to Moses, "See, I make you as God to Pharaoh; and Aaron your brother shall be your prophet. You shall speak all that I command you; and Aaron your brother shall tell Pharaoh."

(iii) It was expected of the Messiah that He would be a prophet. In Matthew 13:57 Jesus characterizes Himself as a prophet, albeit in a proverb, "A prophet is not without honour except in his own country and in his own house." His contemporaries defined His role as that of prophet (Matt 16:14; Luke 7:16; 24:19; John 4:19), and His enemies only brought up weak arguments against this claim (John 7:52; Luke 7:39). Like the Old Testament prophets, Jesus had visions, for example Luke 4:5 when He saw all the kingdoms of the world in a moment; Luke 10:18 where He saw Satan falling from heaven; and at His transfiguration, when some of the disciples were even able to participate in a vision He had. According to John 12:28, Jesus heard the voice of God, and in verse 29 it says the people heard it as well, and interpreted it in different ways. Also in Luke 3:22 at His baptism God speaks directly to Him. At the transfiguration Jesus speaks with Moses and Elijah (Matt 17:3), while the voice of God is directed at the disciples (v 5). But most prophecies are spoken under direct inspiration. This is especially evident at the cursing of the fig tree (Matt 21:19) and in the disputations with the scribes and pharisees (e.g. Luke 11:46f). As God forced Balaam in the Old Testament, so in the New He causes one of the enemies of Jesus, the high priest Caiaphas, to prophesy. In John 11:51 it says of him, "He did not say this of his own accord, but being high priest that year he prophesied that Jesus should die for the nation."

(iv) In Joel 2:28,29 we encounter the promise that the prophetic spirit would one day be poured out on all the people of God. Peter sees the beginning of the fulfilment of this prophecy on the day of Pentecost, when he says, "But this is what was spoken by the prophet Joel: 'And in the last days it shall be, God declares, that I will pour out my Spirit upon all flesh, and your sons and your daughters shall prophesy, and your young men shall see visions, and your old men shall dream dreams; yea, and on my menservants and my maidservants in those days I will pour out my Spirit; and they shall prophesy" (Acts 2:16–18). In the book of Acts it is reported in numerous places that members of the church had visions, e.g., Ananias (Acts 9:10f), Cornelius (10:3f), Paul (16:9f) etc. Visions are particularly common in the Revelation of John.[11]

When Paul says in Galatians 1:12, "For I did not receive it from man, nor was I taught it, but it came through a revelation of Jesus Christ," or in Ephesians 3:3,6 "... how the mystery was made known to me by revelation . . . that is, how the Gentiles are fellow heirs, members of the same body, and partakers of the promise in Christ Jesus," it is likely that he received such revelations through hearing the voice of God directly. That Paul heard the voice of God is apparent from 2 Corinthians 12:4. In Acts 27:23f an angel of God spoke to Paul. Ananias, Peter, and Cornelius also heard the voice of God. In 1 Corinthians 14:24f the spontaneous utterances spoken of are when a prophet speaks directly to a concrete congregational situation. The content of the prophecies of the Old Testament and of Jesus and his followers is normally threefold: presentation of a situation and its evaluation, a look into the future, and directives for the hearer. This is particularly the case in the letters to the seven churches in the book of Revelation.[12] Today as well, the church as the body of Christ shares in the prophetic spirit of Jesus. It becomes manifest in the church in the gift of prophecy.

(g) *The Discerning of Spirits*

(i) The gift of discerning spirits gives to the church and its members the ability to distinguish between divine, human and demonic powers.

(ii) This gift was especially needed in the Old Testament to distinguish the true prophets from the false. Jeremiah says for example, "the prophets prophesy falsely" (5:31), and in Lamentations 2:14 he says, "Your prophets have seen for you false and deceptive visions; they have not exposed your iniquity to restore your fortunes, but have seen for you oracles false and misleading." In Micah 3:11 we read, "its prophets divine for money." A very clear example is portrayed in 1 Kings 22 where the prophet Micaiah takes a stand against the official court prophets, and brands the prophet Zedekiah as false. A real

45

struggle ensues in which Micaiah can only prove the truth of his statements by affirming their certain fulfilment in the future. In doing this he was resorting to an accepted criterion in Israel, alluded to in Jeremiah 28:9, for example.

(iii) Jesus discerned spirits when he exposed as demonic, pious sounding phrases such as "You are the holy one of God," or "Jesus thou Son of the most High God". He would not let Himself be misled by the good counsel of Peter in Matthew 16 and answers, "you are not on the side of God, but of men." Because the Pharisees did not have the gift of discerning spirits they classed workings of the Spirit of God as demonic (Luke 11:15).

(iv) In the church that comes into being after Easter, individual disciples of Jesus had the gift of discerning spirits. In Acts 8:20f for example, Peter exposes the wickedness of Simon Magus, and in Acts 5:3 lays bare as "satanic" the deceit of Ananias and Sapphira.[13] In Acts 13:10 Paul recognises that Bar-Jesus is a "son of the devil". In Philippi (Acts 16:17f) he sees that the pious (albeit factually correct) words uttered by the slave girl with the spirit of divination, spring from an evil spirit. The challenge in 1 John 4:1 "test the spirits to see whether they are of God" applies to all Christians. In verses 2 and 3 John gives a criterion to apply, "By this you know the Spirit of God: every spirit which confesses that Jesus Christ has come in the flesh is of God, and every spirit which does not confess Jesus is not of God. This is the spirit of antichrist, of which you heard that it was coming, and now it is in the world already." In James 3:14–17 we are told that divine wisdom can be distinguished from human and godless wisdom: "But if you have bitter jealousy and selfish ambition in your hearts, do not boast and be false to the truth. This wisdom is not such as come down from above, but is earthly, unspiritual, devilish. For where jealousy and selfish ambition exist, there will be disorder and every vile practice. But the wisdom from above is first pure, then peaceable, gentle, open to reason, full of mercy and good fruits, without uncertainty or insincerity."

In 1 Corinthians 2 Paul distinguishes in a similar way between divine, human, and demonic wisdom. In verses 6 and 7 he writes, "Yet among the mature we do impart wisdom, although it is not a wisdom of this age or of the rulers of this age, who are doomed to pass away. But we impart a secret and hidden wisdom of God, which God decreed before the ages for our glorification." (i.e., that we might already participate in the glory that is to come).

People who did not possess the gift of discerning spirits judged the inspired proclamation of Paul to be senseless chatter (Acts 17:18; 2 Cor 10:10).

Note: In the post-apostolic era, the church was dependent on the gift of discerning spirits in distinguishing true from false prophets. It says, for example, in the *Didache*, an early Christian writing from the end of the first century, "Concerning the Apostles and Prophets, act according to the instructions of the gospel: each apostle who comes to you shall be received as if he were the Lord. But he shall not stay longer than a single day, or if it is necessary he may also stay two. If, however, he stays three days, he is a false prophet. If the apostle is journeying further he shall not take anything with him except bread until he finds shelter. If, however, he asks for money he is a false prophet . . . And you shall not test any prophet who speaks in the Spirit. For every sin will be forgiven, but this will not be forgiven. Certainly not everyone who speaks in the Spirit is a prophet, but only he who has the ways of the Lord. By his ways the false prophet will be distinguished from the true. And no prophet when he orders a table in the Spirit shall eat of it (i.e., an *agape*): if he does this he is a false prophet. Any prophet who teaches the truth, but himself does not do what he teaches, is a false prophet."

(h) *"Praying in the Spirit"* ("Speaking in other languages")

(i) In the gift of praying in the Spirit the ascended Lord gives to the members of His church the possibility of expressing the inexpressible and praising God in new languages.

(ii) We cannot establish with certainty whether the people of the Old Testament practised the gift of prayer in the Spirit. Prayer in the Spirit is by its very nature "a pouring out of the heart to God," and there are a number of places where this idea is expressed, for example Psalm 42:4: "These things I remember, as I pour out my soul," Psalm 62:8 "Pour out your heart before him", and Lamentations 2:19 "Pour out your heart like water before the presence of the Lord!" The description of the prayer of Hannah in 1 Samuel 1:12f sounds very much like "prayer in the Spirit". In verse 13 it says "Hannah was speaking in her heart; only her lips moved, and her voice was not heard." If we can draw any conclusions from present day prayer in the Spirit, what is described here is precisely the same thing as the experience of some who have received this gift today, either in their private devotions or at a prayer meeting, i.e., while praying silently in the Spirit, their lips form words but they do not utter any sounds. It is remarkable as well, that Eli thinks Hannah is drunk and says to her, "how long will you be drunken?" The scoffers in Acts 2 came to the same conclusion when the disciples began to speak in new tongues: "They are filled with new wine!" When Hannah says to Eli, "I have drunk neither wine nor strong drink," it reminds one of Peter's answer, "these men are not drunk, as you suppose." Hannah describes her prayer in verse 15 with the words, "I have been pouring out my soul before the Lord." And therewith she describes exactly what happens when "praying in the Spirit." This "prayer in the Spirit" should be distinguished clearly from the ecstatic utterances common to some of the groups of prophets in the Old Testament. These ecstatic prophets probably drew upon the Canaanite Baal cult and they represent an alien note in the biblical record, for example 1 Kings 18:29. There is a description of ecstatic speech in Isaiah 28:7f. In a state of ecstasy these people reel with wine and stagger with strong drink. Their speaking in tongues is a senseless gibberish: zawlazaw zawlazaw — kawlakaw kawlakaw. This ecstatic gibberish is obviously worthless in the eyes of Isaiah. And yet, in his opinion it points forward to a day when God will speak to Israel in a strange language. He says in verse 11, "Nay, but by men of strange lips and with an alien tongue the Lord will speak to this people." That Isaiah was referring to the Assyrians is clear from 33:19, when he describes the Assyrians as, "the people of an obscure speech which you cannot comprehend, stammering in a tongue which you cannot understand."[14] An exceptional case of speaking in a strange language is recorded in Daniel 5:5 and 25. God allows a hand to write words on a wall in a strange language: "MENE, MENE, TEKEL, and PARSIN".[15]

(iii) Whether Jesus "prayed in the Spirit" or not, is a debateable point. There is no incident in the Gospels which could establish it with certainty. There are, nevertheless, various places that support the possibility. According to Carl Schneider the Greek word *stenazein* or *anastenazein*, which means "sighing", "groaning", was a technical term in the Hellenistic world of that day for prayer that did not involve the mind, but was called forth by the Spirit. According to Mark 7:34 and 8:12 Jesus prayed in this way.[16] The first reference is particularly interesting, for here the term "sighing" (*stenazein*) is used, along with *ephata* (the word), when Jesus was healing someone. According to Rudolph Bultmann,[17] *Ephata* is a *rēsis barbarikē*, an expression in a strange language which, according to numerous parallels in the Hellenistic world, was often used in connection with healing the sick or casting out demons.[18]

(iv) According to Mark 16:17, "prayer in other languages" is one of the signs that will follow those who believe in Jesus.

In the book of Acts we encounter praying in new languages at a number of points. Especially in the story of Pentecost when 120 disciples of Jesus are filled with the Holy Spirit and speak in other languages (Acts 2:4). In Acts 10:44f the Holy Spirit fills the household of Cornelius, and they begin to praise God in new languages. In Acts 19:6 it says of the twelve disciples in Ephesus, "And when Paul had laid his hands upon them, the Holy Spirit came on them; and they spoke with tongues." Paul says of himself in 1 Corinthians 14:18, "I thank God that I speak in tongues more than you all." In 2 Corinthians 5:2–4 the word *stenazein* is used of believers in general implying that this form of prayer is normal for Christians. Because of this, Christians are encouraged to "pray in the Spirit" Ephesians 6:18 and Jude 20. Praying in the Spirit includes speaking in various languages (1 Cor 12:10) of men (Acts 2:8–11), or of angels (1 Cor 13:1). Under some circumstances the languages can be understood by those who hear (Acts 2:6). As a rule, however, they are not understood (1 Cor 14:2,9). When a person prays in the Spirit it is true that his understanding is unfruitful (1 Cor 14:14) but he has complete control over the speaking, being able to begin, cease or quieten it at will (1 Cor 14:28). It is prayer with the *spirit* in contrast to prayer with the *mind* (1 Cor 14:14,15, cf Eph 6:18; Jude 20). According to Romans 8:26 we are given this form of prayer because we do not know how to pray as we ought. The content of speaking in tongues is prayer (1 Cor 14:14), thanksgiving (1 Cor 14:16,17), intercession (Rom 8:27; Eph 6:18), declaring the mighty works of God (Acts 2:11; 10:46), speaking to God (1 Cor 14:2).

(i) The Gift of Interpretation

(i) Interpretation is a complementary gift which makes possible and meaningful the use of tongues in the meeting for worship. Interpretation is not an accurate translation nor a commentary on prayer in the Spirit. Rather it is a presentation of the essential content in the mother tongue. The one praying in the Spirit is speaking to God; the interpreter receives his interpretation from God.

(ii) There is no certain proof for the fact that the gift of interpretation occurred in the Old Testament. Kurt Kuhl thinks it possible that in the symbolic action of Zedekiah in 1 Kings 22:11 we are dealing with interpretation.[19] It is reported of Zedekiah that during the prophecy of the false prophets, he made himself horns of iron and said "with these you shall push the Syrians until they are destroyed." If this is truly interpretation then we must assume that the court prophets were prophesying in an unintelligible language (in ecstasy?). This cannot be proved with any certainty.

A different matter is the interpretation in Daniel 5:26f where Daniel interprets the writing on the wall. Here we are dealing with a true interpretation. But what is interpreted is not a prayer in a strange tongue, but a prophecy of judgment. As a rule, prayer in the Spirit in the Old Testament refers to personal prayer in the sense of pouring out one's heart to God, no interpretation being necessary.

(iii) What was true above, also seems to be true for Jesus. He also used prayer in the Spirit alone as a form of personal encounter with His heavenly Father. Because of this there was no need for interpretation. The interpretation of a *rēsis barbarikē* is a later translation by the gospel writer.

(iv) It is only in the church that the gift of interpretation takes on real meaning. Through this gift, prayer in the Spirit becomes significant for the gathered church (1 Cor 14:27). Paul ranks "prayer in the Spirit", when interpreted, as equal in value in building up the church, to prophecy—the most desirable gift (1 Cor 14:5).

The gift of interpretation is given to the one praying in the Spirit (1 Cor 14:5,13) or to another (1 Cor 12:10f; 14:26f). Interpretation is just as much a gift given by the Holy Spirit as prayer in a new language, and does not involve an intellectual understanding of the language used.

What a rich variety of gifts of divine grace! And it must be remembered that the gifts listed in our passage are just a small part of the divine riches in Christ, "All these are inspired by one and the same Spirit, who apportions to each one individually as he wills" (1 Cor 12:11).

With reference to John 7:38f "He who believes in me, as the scripture has said, 'Out of his heart shall flow rivers of living water.' Now this he said about the Spirit, which those who believed in him were to receive", Cyril of Jerusalem (AD 315–386) writes: "Why did Christ name the grace of the Spirit water? Water is contained in everything; plants and animals need water for their life; in the form of rain water comes from heaven. It comes down in that one form, but it then works in many different ways. One and the same spring irrigates the garden, and one and the same rain falls on the whole world. But then it becomes white in the lily, red in the rose, dark yellow in the daffodils and hyacinths. In every variety of colour it appears in such different kinds of things. It takes one form in the palm tree, quite another in the vine. In each it is different, although in itself it is always the same. The rain itself never changes and comes down now in one way, now in another, but it still aims to become the essence of the thing which receives it, and becomes whatever is appropriate to that.

"So it is also with the Holy Spirit, who is one only and undivided but yet gives Himself to each as He will. As wood which was dry, as soon as it absorbs water brings forth twigs, so the soul which has lived in sin as soon as by repentance it has been made worthy of the Holy Spirit, brings forth fruits of righteousness. Although the Holy Spirit is of *one* kind, He nevertheless works, according to the will of God, every variety of virtue. He serves the tongue of one, gives to another the power to drive out devils, enlightens the soul of another to prophesy, bestows on another the gift of interpreting divine scripture. One he strengthens in chastity, another he teaches mercifulness, another fasting and mortification, another contempt of wordly desires, again others he makes martyrs. In one He works in this way, in another in that, although He Himself remains the same."

5

One Body — Many Members
(1 Cor 12 : 12-27)

(a) *The Body of Christ.*

"For just as the body is one and has many members, and all the members of the body, though many, are one body, so it is with Christ"—verse 12.

It is commonly known that in the ancient world such secular structures as, for example, the state, are compared to the functioning of the human body. There are examples of this in Roman, Greek and Jewish literature. Livy (11/32) for example, has Agrippa Menenius tell the Plebians who were on strike, the following parable:

"There was a day when the human body was not as harmoniously ordered as it is today. Every member of the body had its own will and its own language. The other members became angry that they had to concern themselves with the need of the stomach, and provide it with everything. The stomach just remained at the centre of all this satisfied with all that was brought to it. The members made this decision: the hands would not supply any food to the mouth—the mouth would not receive any food nor would the teeth chew. Consequently during this time in which they starved the stomach all the parts of the body became weak and feeble. Then they realized that the role of the stomach was not to be despised as a passive one. Just as he was being nourished, he was passing on strength in return."

Plato writes in his *Republic* (462 c-d):

"When one of us has a wounded finger, the body and soul of the person and their inter-relationship are affected, we say *the man* feels pain in his finger. Even so with every other part of the body— when one part suffers there is pain, and there is joy when one part is restored to health."

The Jewish writer Josephus writes in *The Jewish War* (4/vii/406):

"There was an insurrection among the Jewish provinces. Just as in a body: when one organ is diseased and inflamed, and this happens to be the organ by which the body breathes then the other members are unable to recuperate being destroyed by the same disease."

This image has been much discussed and the extent of its reality argued by many. For a number of other examples and an explanation and examination of the sources of the metaphor see: E. Schweizer *The Church as the Body of Christ*, (London, 1965), J. A. T. Robinson *The Body, a study in Pauline Theology* (London 1957), E. Best *One Body in Christ* (1955) Alan Cole *The Body of Christ* (London, 1964) and an article under *Soma* by E. Schweizer in Kittel's *Wörterbuch*.

In the writings of the extra-canonical authors, the human body is only an image for a social structure. The writer is always aware of the fact that the body only serves as an image and has no independent reality in itself. It is the human group which is the primary reality. The society described is *like* a body.

It is a different matter in the writings of Paul. He does not say that the Christian church is like Christ's body, but "you *are* the body of Christ" (v. 27). The body is a reality. Christians are not like members of any body, but are, according to their very nature, members of a specific body, the body of Christ. In order to accomplish His work while on earth, Jesus had a body made of flesh and blood. In order to accomplish

His work today, Jesus has a body that consists of living human beings. According to some manuscripts Paul says in Ephesians 5:30 that we are bone of His bone, and flesh of His flesh.

During his earthly life Jesus could do as much as His body allowed. He was limited by weariness, hunger, thirst, temptation, etc. Today Jesus is able to do as much on earth as His present body, i.e., His church, permits. "In our day Jesus does nothing independently of the church nor can the church do anything independently of Christ" (Max Thurian). Today the church causes Christ much sorrow through disunity, selfish pride, wilfulness, disobedience, deadness, etc. Jesus works on the earth today only through His church. Jesus will act in proportion to the harmony which exists between Himself and His church. Jesus is prepared to do all, to grant all, to exercise His authority, and to triumph victoriously wherever the church allows Him to work.

The linguistic expert Frank Laubach writes: "When Christ was here on earth, He was limited to performing His ministry in one place and at one time. He was one man, walking beside one sea in one little corner of the earth. He healed whoever He touched, but His touch was necessarily limited by time and by space. Now, does it make sense that the Father would send His Son for this limited ministry? I don't think that is tenable. He made provision to carry on the work through the Holy Spirit: we are to complete His mission. We are His multiplied hands, His feet, His voice and compassionate heart. Imperfect and partial to be sure, but His healing Body just the same. And it is through the Holy Spirit (Christ's love which is everywhere at once), that we receive the power to carry on the work of the apostles. It is a challenging and sobering thought: when we receive the Holy Spirit into our lives, we receive the same urgent and life-giving force that led our Master."

(b) *How do I become a member of the Body of Christ?*

"For by one Spirit we were all baptized into one body—Jews or Greeks, slaves or free—and all were made to drink of one Spirit" verse 13.

Through participation in the one Spirit I become a member of the one Body. Before people can participate in this Spirit, they are bound to national, cultural, social, and religious groups of all kinds. Participation in the one Spirit transcends all these human ties and binds those who possess the Spirit in the body of Christ. This new relationship is stronger than all previous ties. The basis of all other ties are related either to the *body* (e.g., race, colour, etc.) or to the *soul* (e.g., culture, religion, etc.). But the members of the body of Christ participate in the one *Spirit*. In using the expression "baptize" and "drink", Paul makes it clear that the act of receiving the Spirit can be viewed from various aspects. The expression "baptize" always means "to be dipped or immersed into something". The Spirit surrounds and covers the believer as water does at baptism. The expression "drink", however, gives the impression that the believer receives the Spirit into himself as he does the bread and wine at the Lord's Supper. The believer is "in the Spirit" and the Spirit is "in the believer" (compare this to the parallel expressions Paul uses "we are in Christ" and "Christ is in us"). In both cases the form of the verb in Greek suggests that receiving the Spirit is a single experience which happened at a specific time in the past. That Paul uses the expressions "baptize" and "drink" in connection with receiving the Spirit, throws some light on Baptism and the Lord's Supper. As the individual member is bound inwardly to the body of Christ, so also through Baptism and Communion the body of Christ is represented outwardly. We must not, however, divide the body of Christ between inward and outward. We cannot distinguish between the visible and invisible church. We cannot relegate the evils in the church to the "visible" church. We should be concerned much more that there should be no discrepancy between the outward signs and the inward reality. Jesus does not permit us to destroy the signs. Whoever undermines the symbol is at the same time destroying a part of the thing itself. In 1 Corinthians 11:29f Paul makes it clear that an indifferent observance of the Lord's Supper results in a sickly body of Christ. The purpose of Baptism and the Lord's Supper are one: "To be drawn into the mighty stream of what the Spirit is doing" (K. Heim).

Verse 14, "For the body does not consist of one member but of many." After Paul has said in verse 13 that those who were divided have been welded together into one body after receiving the Spirit, he emphasizes in verse 14 that the body is made up of many different members. Unity and diversity are inextricably interwoven. Through receiving the Spirit I become not only a member of the *one body*, but I become a *special member* of that body, i.e., I receive a function that is altogether unique and personal. All organic life manifests diversity. Divine unity is never uniform and monotonous, always diverse and varied. Every Christian is original and unique. I miss my own commission if I copy others. Thereby I become an imitation instead of an original. Every Christian has his own commission, his own gift (cf. 1 Cor 12:7-11; Rom 12:5-18; Eph 4:11-16; 1 Pet 4:10).

(c) *Against Inferiority Feelings*
  (i) *The Complaint*

"If the foot should say, 'Because I am not a hand, I do not belong to the body', that would not make it any less a part of the body. And if the ear should say, 'Because I am not an eye, I do not belong to the body', that would not make it any less a part of the body." Verses 15, 16.

Where gifts are distributed, some may be dissatisfied. They glance longingly at the apparently superior gifts of others. They feel a little slighted because they have not received one of the more coveted gifts. There are some Christians who seem to think that they hardly belong to the body, because in their own eyes they have received a lesser gift. They say: "I am *only* a foot—now if I were a *hand* then I would really represent something. A hand is much better than a foot and much more useful to the body." Or else they say: "I am only an ear—if I were an eye, then I would *be* something. An eye is much nicer than an ear and is much more useful to the body." The less honourable, unpresentable members of the body, desire to be something better. The foot and ear feel inferior. This is how "Corinthians" in all ages of the church have felt. "I only have the gift of service—now, if I had the gift of speaking in a new language, I would really amount to something." "I only have the gift of spiritual counselling; if I had the gift of healing the sick, then I really would be something."

(ii) *The Answer to this Complaint*
1. *Variety is necessary*

"If the whole body were an eye, where would be the hearing? If the whole body were an ear, where would be the sense of smell? If all were a single organ, where would the body be? As it is, there are many parts, yet one body." Verses 17, 19, 20.

Coveting the gifts of others denies completely the very nature of the body. It is childish, self-centred thinking. The body would be destroyed if it consisted of eyes or ears. With a touch of humour Paul suggests what a grotesque monster such a body would be! One cannot imagine what a body would be if it consisted only of one member. The variety among members is necessary and ought to be a source of joy to the Christian. Whoever is jealous of the gifts of others is sinning against his brother. Instead of envious sidelong glances we ought to rejoice at the gifts of others. We ought to pray that all the gifts should be present in our congregation in abundance (1 Cor 1:5-7), realizing then that *which* member exercises which gift is quite unimportant as long as the body is healthy and growing. But it *is* important that the one body becomes visible and recognizable by the variety present among its members.

2. *"God arranges ..."*

"But as it is, God arranged the organs in the body, each one of them, as he chose." Verse 18.

Whoever envies his brother for his gift, is not only sinning against his brother but also against God, for God has appointed according to His will, a place and a function for each member of the body of Christ. The seeming ignorance of God is still wiser than the greatest of man's wisdom. He knows exactly which function suits us best and in which way we can best serve the total body. Envious glances at the gift of another is one way of calling into question the wisdom of God and criticizing His actions.

(d) *Against Pride*
(i) *The Attitude of the Arrogant*

"The eye cannot say to the hand, 'I have no need of you', nor again the head to the feet, 'I have no need of you.'" Verse 21.

Naturally, all this can also be reversed: the apparently "better" members can look with disdain on the apparently "inferior" members. The eye says to the hand: "What are you in comparison to me. I can manage without you. I can see the light and have apprehended the truth." The head says to the feet: "What are you in comparison to me. I can get along without you." And the "Corinthian" healer today says: "I have the gift of healing, I don't need anyone else. My commission is the most important." And then he launches out conducting mass meetings, and one through whom Christ wanted to make His complete salvation visible, often causes untold damage. The present day "Corinthian" ascetic says: "I can live alone. I do not need the others." He moves into isolation and leads a holy life all by himself, thereby robbing the church of an important contribution. In the light of the New Testament it is not possible for an individual member or even an élite group of members to sever itself from the total body of Christ to live unto itself. For as a result the total church is robbed of some important functions. Naturally it is easier, especially at a place where there is lack of understanding or considerable friction, to go one's own way without regard to the others. But such an attitude is a crime against the body of Christ. According to 2 Corinthians 11:24 Paul received the thirty-nine strokes five times. In his day this punishment was carried out when a person who deserved to be excommunicated from the synagogue desired to remain. The Jews apparently, would have preferred to see Paul establish a little "Christian" society of his own. But Paul knew that he was integrally bound to the people of God of old and consequently allowed himself to be whipped within an inch of his life rather than forsake the "church". And he also knew himself bound in loyalty to the total body of Christians; so much so, that according to Galatians 2:2 he would have considered his work "in vain" if it had threatened the unity of the church.

(ii) *The Answer to the Proud*
1. *The so-called "better" members need the "lesser" ones*

"On the contrary, the parts of the body which seem to be weaker are indispensable." Verse 22.

In the Livy parable, the proud hands, mouth, and teeth refused to serve the useless stomach, until they began to suffer as a result. Then they realized that the stomach also had an important and useful function and that they could not exist without it.

Clement of Rome, writing to the church at Corinth towards the close of the first century says (1/37):

"Consider how orderly, willing and obedient soldiers are in fulfilling their service to the government. Not everyone is a commander or a captain over a thousand, a hundred, or over fifty, but everyone carries out the orders of the king at the post to which he has been assigned. The greater cannot do without the lesser nor the lesser without the greater. There is a certain mixture in all things, and therein lies its usefulness. Take our body, for example: the head is dependent on the feet and the feet on the head; even the least significant members of our body are essential for the proper functioning of the whole; as they agree and submit to one another they maintain the body."

2. *The more presentable members have to serve the less presentable ones*

"And those parts of the body which we think less honourable we invest with the greater honour, and our unpresentable parts are treated with greater modesty, which our more presentable parts do not require. But God has so adjusted the body, giving the greater honour to the inferior part." Verses 23, 24.

The more unpresentable parts call for more adequate clothing than is required for the more presentable parts. In the church as well, the unpresentable members are to be honoured in a special way. Consequently the attitude of the world is reversed. Jesus said: "You know that those who are supposed to rule over the Gentiles lord it over them, and their great men exercise authority over them. But it shall not be so among you; but whoever would be great among you must be your servant and whoever would be first among you must be slave of all. For the Son of man also came not to be served but to serve, and to give his life as a ransom for many." (Mark 10:42–45; cf. Matt 23:11; Mark 9:35; Luke 14:11; John 13:3–17; 1 Cor 1:27; James 2:5).

In the church, for example, the true apostle proves himself precisely by his readiness to serve, to be whipped, persecuted and slandered for the church (1 Cor 4:9; 2 Cor 11:23f; Col 1:24). Jesus proved He was sent of God by serving and laying down His life; and the same kind of selfless service is expected of the true apostle. The false apostle is detected by his desire for honour and power. The variety of functions are not given to the individual for his own glorification. The gifts are not, in the first place, given to the one who ministers them, but to the one who is ministered to. It is, for example, the sick person that recovers, who receives healing as a gift, not the one who lays hands on him and prays for healing. According to Romans 1:11 Paul wanted to "impart" his gift to the Romans, i.e., he wants to give them gifts by exercising his God-appointed function in the body of Christ.

Who can be spoken of now as having the great or the small gift? The one who ministers or the one who receives? The one speaking or the one listening? This cannot be established for the body is one. All gifts and services are functions of the one body. The body is thoroughly "mixed" (1 Clement: "There is a certain mixture in all things and their usefulness is contained therein").

(e) *The Body of Christ as an indissoluble Fellowship*

"... that there may be no discord in the body, but that the members may have the same care for one another. If one member suffers, all suffer together; if one member is honoured, all rejoice together." Verses 25, 26.

The body is so well integrated that the questions of great and small gifts or presentable and unpresentable parts really do not arise. A disintegration into solitary members is no longer possible for they all care for one another. Whenever this is not in a congregation, the nature of the body of Christ has not yet been grasped. The members of such a congregation are still in the infant stage (1 Cor 3:1f; cf. also the two first sentences in Livy's parable. In some congregations one would have to quote these sentences in the present tense).

All the members of the body of Christ are inextricably involved together, for better or for worse, for growth or for decay. Whoever becomes a part of the body of Christ can no longer separate himself from his brothers. The body of Christ is an indissoluble fellowship from which there is no easy escape. "If one member suffers we all suffer." If there are members not prepared to suffer with him who suffers, others must suffer all the more—including suffering for *their* self-centredness and unwillingness to suffer. As a Christian I cannot rejoice about my own spiritual condition if my brother next to me is prostrate in sin or sickness. It is irrational to imagine that the illness of another member has nothing to do with my own health. As Josephus put it: "If one member of a body is sick and enflamed . . . the other members cannot recuperate, for they share in the illness." We cannot say, "I'm not concerned when my finger is not well; I'm healthy," but have to admit rather, that I suffer when my finger suffers (see Plato's comparison above). In Livy's parable as well, all the members suffer when the stomach suffers. The reverse is also true: when one organ, for example the stomach, functions particularly well, it profits them all. If one member exercises great authority in spiritual counselling, in healing, or in evangelism, the whole body profits. "If one member is honoured, all rejoice together."

If one member rejoices about the other, then the body of Christ functions well, and Christ can accomplish His work unhindered, and can make many happy. "Now you are the body of Christ and individually members of it" (1 Cor 12:27).

6

Charisma and Offices

(1 Cor 12 : 28-30)

"And God has appointed in the church first apostles, second prophets, third teachers, then workers of miracles, then healers, helpers, administrators, speakers in various kinds of tongues. Are all apostles? Are all prophets? Are all teachers? Do all work miracles? Do all possess gifts of healing? Do all speak with tongues? Do all interpret?"

In verse 28 Paul leads the discussion to the charismatic functions of individual members. The statement: One body—many members, is further concretized by the expression: One congregation—many services (ministries). In verse 28 Paul is concerned not so much with individuals and their gifts as he is with ministries within the congregation—and the Church at large. Paul links verse 28 with verse 18 when he says, "God has appointed . . ." The exercise of a ministry in the church is not based on personal desire, for God has appointed the talents according to His will (cf. the parable of Jesus, Matt 25:14f and Luke 19:12f). Having apportioned them, He expects us to work with them. In making his list Paul differentiates between (a) people: apostles, prophets, teachers, and (b) activities: mighty works, healings, administrations, leading, speaking in other languages.

There are two things worth noting in this list, (a) Paul does differentiate between offices and gifts; (b) Paul does *not* differentiate between natural and supernatural gifts. In doing this the list represents a link between 1 Corinthians 12:8–10 and Romans 12 and Ephesians 4.

(a) *Offices in the New Testament*
It is taken for granted in the New Testament that besides gifts, which are given to *all*, there are special ministries given to individual Christians to fulfil. The early church differentiated between congregational ministries (overseers, elders, servants) and inter-congregational ministries (apostles, prophets, evangelists, pastors, teachers). We will deal here only with the ministries mentioned in our text.

(i) *Apostles*
Vincent Taylor differentiates four groups of apostles in the New Testament[1]

1. The apostles in Jerusalem (the Twelve and James the brother of Jesus). The conditions of their apostleship are mentioned in Acts 1:21f.
2. The apostles from Antioch (Paul, Barnabas, Silvanus). It was their special responsibility to shepherd the Gentile churches.
3. Apostles with localized responsibilities among the Gentiles (e.g., Andronicus and Junias, cf. 2 Cor 8:23 ". . . and as for our brethren, they are apostles of the churches").
4. Apostolic ministries (e.g., Timothy and Titus carried out certain apostolic services without ever being referred to specifically in the New Testament as "apostles").

The sign common to all apostles, as Taylor sees it, is, "They must have been conscious of an inner call from Christ, to which the Holy Spirit bore unmistakable testimony, and their call was recognized and endorsed by the church."[2]

The New Testament gives us a particularly good insight into

the apostolic office of Paul. Four obvious marks appear:
1. Called by God—Galatians 1:15f.
2. Singled out by the church—Acts 13:1f.
3. Recognized by the church at large—Galatians 2:7f.
4. Confirmed by apostolic signs—2 Corinthians 12:12.
These four things are certainly typical for all apostles.

In answer to the question whether there are still apostles today, Ralf Luther says in his New Testament word book[3]: "Christ did not have only twelve apostles. The New Testament shows us apostles in all churches (Eph 4:11; 1 Cor 12:28), men empowered to maintain or bring to birth the relationships between Christ and His churches.

"The apostolic office in the New Testament is not an exceptional arrangement necessary for only one special time, but rather a normal ministry which is always needed (even if the Twelve do have a unique significance). If there are no apostles, i.e., none who are divinely commissioned, authorized and empowered, then the relationships between heaven and earth are severed."

In fact, there is no place in the New Testament which implies that the apostolic office was designed only for the first generation of the church's existence. On the contrary, in the history of the church we repeatedly encounter apostles (e.g., Ansgar, apostle to the North). Calvin maintains in his Institutes[4], that God calls forth apostles "as they are needed at different times" (*prout temporum necessitas postulat*).

(ii) *Prophets*
Besides those who received the charisma of prophecy, there were also those Christians in the early church who had the special office of prophet e.g., Judas and Silas (Acts 15:32f) or Agabus (11:27f; 21:10). Eduard Schweizer writes[5]: "Their

service is everywhere regarded as a direct gift of the Spirit; and the Church no more chooses prophets than it chooses apostles. It can recognize them, and it also has to test them . . ."

Paul Tillich gives this answer to the question as to whether there are still prophets today[6]: "For the prophetic spirit has not disappeared from the earth. Decades before the world wars, men judged the European civilization and prophesied its end in speech and print. There are among us people like these. They are like the refined instruments which register the shaking of the earth on far-removed sections of its surface. These people register the shaking of their civilization, its self-destructive trends, and its disintegration and fall, decades before the final catastrophe occurs. They have an invisible and almost infallible sensorium in their souls; and they have an irresistible urge to pronounce what they have registered, perhaps against their own wills. For no true prophet has ever prophesied voluntarily. It has been forced upon him by a Divine Voice to which he has not been able to close his ears. No man with a prophetic spirit likes to foresee and foresay the doom of his own period. It exposes him to a terrible anxiety within himself, to severe and often deadly attacks from others, and to the charge of pessimism and defeatism on the part of the majority of the people. Men desire to hear good tidings; and the masses listen to those who bring them. All the prophets of the Old and New Testaments, and others during the history of the Church, had the same experience. They all were contradicted by the false prophets, who announced salvation when there was no salvation."

(iii) *Teachers*

Besides prophets, we also encounter teachers, for example in the church at Antioch (Acts 13:1f). Besides the charisma of a word of knowledge, these men also had to have the gift of teaching (1 Cor 12:28). Certainly a man like Apollos of Alexandria had the office of a teacher (Acts 18:24f; 1 Cor 3:6), along with those mentioned in Acts 13. God expects the teacher to fulfil his office faithfully (Rom 12:7; 2 Tim 4:2). The day will come when they will have to give an account of themselves (James 3:1). According to Ephesians 4:11 the office of teacher and that of shepherd (pastor) are closely related. Jerome, one of the early fathers, said: "Whoever is a shepherd, must be a teacher."

(b) "Natural" and "Supernatural" Gifts

In the list of gifts in verse 28, besides the gifts mentioned in 1 Corinthians 12:8-10 (miracles, speaking in tongues), two new gifts of divine grace appear: helpers and administrators. According to recently discovered papyri the Greek word for administration (*antilepsis*) was a technical term in the field of banking and referred to the chief accountant. In other words, we are concerned here with administration of money. The expression *kybernesis* (leading or piloting duties) was adopted as the foreign word *cybernetics* into the vocabulary of business. It refers to the leader of a business, the "manager" so to speak.[7]

So the ministry of administration and leadership responsibility are charismatic services. This confirms the fact that Paul knew no distinction between natural and supernatural gifts, between ordinary and extraordinary ministries. For him, all the activities of a Christian are saturated with the Spirit of God.

W. Hollenweger writes in this connection:[8] "The whole distinction between natural and supernatural is outdated, both scientifically and theologically, and can no longer be seriously advocated. Scientifically it is no longer possible to delineate the boundaries of what was called 'natural'. On the basis of statistical measurement, assumptions based on a high degree of possibility can be made, concerning the relationship of certain forces and substances. But no modern scientist would claim to know the total body of facts and forces that lead to a certain result. He must always reckon with the possibility of discovering new factors not yet known to him. He will, nevertheless, stick to the principle that all factors can be known, even though he knows that every new discovery creates as many new problems as it solves old ones. It is because of this, though, that the scientist knows it is impossible to establish with absolute certainty the boundary in a theological sense, of the "natural". He will always maintain that there is no point in this world at which the natural comes to an end— even if he cannot describe all of nature yet.

"From the theological standpoint as well, it is irresponsible to describe the supernatural as a breaking through of natural laws. The image of Himself that God allows to arise out of the natural world is not to be identified with the witness of scripture—remembering that the knowledge of so-called natural laws is in a constant state of flux and that a theology which limits itself to the so-called direct inbreak of God into the inexplainable is constantly fighting a rearguard action. And besides this, Paul does not distinguish between natural and supernatural in terms of phenomenological categories. Marriage and celibacy, administrative gifts such as leadership, service responsibilities such as the diaconate, as well as healing through prayer, speaking in other languages, and prophecy are all put into the same category and are reckoned to be *charisma* (cf. Rom 12 especially). The fact that a manifestation is extraordinary does in no way prove that it is charismatic, nor is it suspect because of this—a practice that seems to be common in the church today. Phenomenological, aesthetic, and psychological categories have no part to play in the evaluation of the gifts.

"What are the distinguishing marks of a genuine gift? Paul suggests three criteria: (a) it must be "for the common good" (*pros to sympheron*), (b) it dare not work in a way that contradicts the Incarnation, (c) it must help to establish and express the Lordship of Christ. Everything must measure itself by this. If a sermon is not 'for the common good', then the gift of prophecy has not arisen. If a hymn or newspaper article is *pros to sympheron* then it has been a gift. How the sermon is born—whether through fourteen days of intensive study and meditation or through a sudden inspiration—is unimportant. What is important is the consequences it calls forth."

If we were called upon to attempt a definition of charisma it might be: a gift is manifested when being set free by the Holy Spirit, my natural endowments blossom forth glorifying Christ and building up His church.

There is no *Christian* action that is independent of the Holy Spirit. In practical terms this means, for example, that for the Christian doctor his total activity is charismatic activity. A prescription or an innoculation are only different ways of laying on hands. Both are done prayerfully and in fellowship with Jesus. Because he knows that God is the one who heals, he will use his medical skill in utter dependence upon God.

Striving in Love
(1 Cor 12 : 31)

Verse 31 is usually translated: "But earnestly desire the higher gifts. And I will show you a still more excellent way."

This translation is not without its problems. In his research on this verse, Gerhard Iber[1] maintains that it is hardly likely that Paul would encourage them to strive selfishly after the greatest gifts after he has just admonished them to be content with the gift apportioned to them (cf. 1 Cor 12:12f). The trouble in Corinth was precisely that everybody wanted to be the hand or the eye (1 Cor 12:15,16). They were distinguishing between greater and lesser gifts. Everybody was coveting the so-called "greater" gifts! There was no apparent reason why Paul should strengthen them in this unspiritual striving. As far as he could see it was their childish immaturity that made them want the "greatest" gifts. Verse 31, consequently, ought to be translated: "*You are striving* after the greatest gifts" (the Greek form of the verb here can be translated in the indicative or the imperative). That this translation is correct is confirmed by 14:12, where Paul characterizes the Corinthians as people who strive after gifts.

Iber suggests: "The verse then characterizes the attitude of the Corinthian church and expresses succinctly the cause for the apostle's rebuke: that they were striving after the 'greatest' gifts."[2] Which were the gifts that they sought after so eagerly? Most likely the ones that Paul just mentioned, and of which he said: Not all are apostles, and not all are prophets, etc. So in

Corinth everybody wanted to be an apostle, prophet, teacher, disregarding the fact that the gifts which involve an office necessitate a special call from God. The prominent gifts of a more miraculous nature are also sought after: the working of mighty deeds, gifts of healing, speaking in other languages and interpretation of these languages.

The gifts mentioned just before these, were apparently not sought after: the administration of finances, and interestingly enough the gift of leadership. It seems they were all trying to avoid responsibility. With a touch of irony Paul continues in verse 31: "Since you have excelled yourselves in *striving* after the great gifts, then let me show you an even more excellent way." There are, in other words, two ways of receiving and manifesting gifts: by *striving* after them or by attaining them through *love*.

In loving my neighbour, I unconsciously give him what others might call a gift. In chapter 14 it looks as if both ways are recognized: "Make love your aim and earnestly desire the spiritual gifts." Iber states: "There were certain things that Paul could not say before chapter 13 for they would have resulted then, in a wrong tendency in the church. This could only be restrained and restored to its proper perspective when the context and measure of the gifts, as dealt with in chapter 13, is taken into account. Only then could Paul dare to encourage the Corinthians to 'strive after spiritual gifts'."[3]

These two forms of striving in love are expressed in 14:12 in this way: "Since you are eager for manifestations of the Spirit, strive to excel in building up the church."

Love, therefore, is not a gift. Nor is it the greatest gift (cf. 1 Cor 12:31). The expression *charisma* is never used in the New Testament to describe love. According to Galatians 5 love is a fruit of the Spirit—one might say *the* fruit of the

Spirit.[4] Love is also no alternative to the gifts. According to 1 Corinthians 14:1 love and gifts are both to be sought after.[5]

Love is the principle of applying the gifts. It lies at the very heart of all gifts; it is the life-blood of the body of Christ.[6] Love is the immanence of Jesus in His body the church. The gifts of divine grace are all channels and ways through which love can and does manifest itself.

L. Christenson illustrates this point in the following way: "Imagine a man who is dying of thirst in the desert and a rescue party is sent out. They set out with hearts full of love and compassion for him. They find him. His tongue and lips are swollen. 'Water, water' he gasps desperately. They, however, go over to him and embrace him saying, 'Dear brother, I don't believe in gifts—just in love.' That is outrageous, is it not? The gifts of the Spirit are no second rate alternative to love. They are the means the Spirit gives us to express the love of Christ in all concrete and practical ways."[7] But love not only expresses itself in gifts, it also at the same time controls all the gifts. Ernst Käsemann says: "Practicality is the presupposition of right ministry and of that *agape* which is the costlier way because it sets bounds to the ego."[8]

PART II
CHAPTER THIRTEEN

8

Gifts without Love are Useless
(1 Cor 13 : 1-3)

(a) Liturgy without Love

"If I speak in the tongues of men and of angels, but have no love, I am a noisy gong or a clanging cymbal." Verse 1.

Paul assumes that speaking in tongues means speaking in human or angelic languages. According to 2 Corinthians 12:4 and Revelation 14:2f, angelic languages are unutterable. Paul means that even if he could speak in perfect Greek or Chinese, or could speak an angelic language (which is really unutterable), the exercise of this gift without love (i.e., for self-glorification) would be as a clanging cymbal. (He is here referring to ancient single toned musical instruments which cannot produce a melody). Love is choked "where a few of those who claim to excel in the gifts are ostentatious in their prayers and utterances, and spread their wings, leaving behind in spiritual isolation all the seekers and the uninitiated."[1]

(b) Knowledge and Faith without Love

"And if I have prophetic powers, and understand all mysteries and all knowledge, and if I have all faith, so as to remove mountains, but have not love, I am nothing." Verse 2.

That the exercise of gifts without love is worthless, is not only true of praying in the Spirit, but also of prophecy, the revelation of mysteries (cf. Rom 16:25), knowledge, and mountain-moving faith. W. Hollenweger writes: "This judgment includes prophecy as theological thought and reflection as well as instantaneous knowledge. What matters is not the manner in which the knowledge is made manifest but that which is accomplished by it."[2]

(c) *Service and Martyrdom without Love*

"If I give away all I have, and if I deliver my body to be burned, but have not love, I gain nothing." Verse 3.

According to verse 3 something can appear on the surface to be the highest act of love and yet can be loveless. The literal Greek states: "To convert all my possessions into bits of bread for the hungry." In practical terms, this means feeding the hungry as Christ commanded in Matthew 25:31f. It becomes clear, here, that there are two ways of fulfilling Christ's commandment to love: an outward, legalistic way (consequently selfish) which is worthless in the eyes of Jesus and a second way that lavishes itself upon Jesus. This twofold way of giving is illustrated in the New Testament in John 12:1–8 in the attitudes of Judas and Mary. Martyrdom *can* be an expression of the highest love towards God, and it *has* certainly often been this. Jesus says in John 15:13, "Greater love has no man than this, that a man lay down his life for his friends." But there is also a type of martyrdom that springs from the desire always to be right and to stick fanatically to one's own ideas. The outsider will certainly not be able to determine what kind of martyrdom it was. In the eyes of God, bold witness, if still centred in the self, is of no value.

Summary:

Verses 1–3 are not concerned with the appearance of a brilliant gift, but with its function. This is the decisive question:

Is *love* translated into deed through this *charisma* or not? Does the neighbour encounter the ascended Lord in the gift or just the man exercising the gift? Is Christ incarnate being glorified and lifted up or does the gift serve to glorify man? Gifts are functions of the body of Christ. They are His eyes, hands and feet with which He acts and moves on earth. When gifts are no longer an expression of Christ's actions, then they are not only useless but harmful in their effect. They are counterfeits which offer my neighbour nothing, but positively deceive him.

9

The Nature of Love
(1 Cor 13: 4-7)

Paul describes the relationship between charisma and love in the 13th chapter of his first letter to the Corinthians. Especially in verses 4-7, he describes the essence of love, painted against the dark background of selfishness and mistrust. Since love is *the* essential quality of all education, we shall consider these verses in detail.

"Love is patient and kind." Verse 4a.

These two expressions could serve as a title for this whole section.[1] They describe love according to its breadth and its depth or quality. Love is patient. The literal meaning is: it has great breadth and capacity; or as some translators put it: love "suffers long." That means: its patience never runs out. It is the love of the waiting father in the parable of the lost son, Luke 15; it endures, where we would have given up. It is the love for which there are no hopeless cases.

The quality of this love is friendliness itself; not a weak form of kindness but a strong kind of love. Behind the Greek word lies the thought of thoroughness and usefulness. Because love is strong in its kindness, it can afford to approach another with kindness, even if that other is not kindly disposed in return. Love has nothing to fear. In what follows Paul describes love using a variety of expressions. He does not describe love in abstract nouns but shows in verbs how the loving person reacts in concrete situations.

(1) *The Trial experienced by the Christian because of the Darkness within himself.*

"Love does not behave jealously. Love does not brag, it does not puff up, it does not act unbecomingly. Love does not seek its own." Verses 4b-5a.

These five negated verbs point to five dangers the Christian encounters in himself

(a) *Love does not behave jealously*

The first danger is jealousy. There was a party spirit in evidence in Corinth. There were those set on pushing forward their own particular set of ideas. Wherever gifts are exercised the danger exists that I will want to hold the stage with my prophecy, my knowledge, my discernment of spirits. Such a selfish desire for recognition severs itself from love. If God grants knowledge or prophecy, etc., as a spiritual gift, He is also concerned that the gift produces the right effect. I do not have to defend God's cause; and certainly not my own! As in every aspect of the Christian life, Christ is our great example here, for He entrusted everything to God (1 Pet 2:23). If love is real, one does not have to fight jealously for "God's" cause, which is quite often one's own cause!

(b) *Love does not brag*

The second danger is boasting. The person who boasts or brags, may be speaking the truth, but his manner of speech is not in keeping with this truth. If God does something — wonderfully healing a sick person for instance — it is not in keeping with this act to blare it out for all the world to hear. Only powers hostile to God are concerned with blowing trumpets

(Mark 1:24,34; Acts 16:17f). That which proceeds from God moves forward quietly (Matt 17:1). So love does not brag. Love does not gossip about sensational miracles, visions, prophecies, etc. When God manifests a gift in a concrete situation it is the edified person, who has been helped by the gift, who remains, not the action by which he was helped. If the deed (charisma) is talked about in a sensational way, then one is guilty of boasting. In 1 Thessalonians 1:9, Paul records that the *others* (= the unbelievers) report "how you turned to God from the idols to serve a living and true God." If the *others* see nothing, then it is ridiculous when we blow our trumpet. Love does not brag.

(c) *Love does not puff up*

The third danger is puffing up. The Greek word *physao* means "blowing". It is a loud-sounding word derived from the root *phu* (the noun *physa* means "bellow"). If I blow something up I am making more of it than corresponds to the actual facts; I am exaggerating. When you blow a balloon up it becomes bigger and at the same time more easily deflated. When God does something, there is always the danger that we do not consider it quite enough and we are tempted to puff it up a little more to make it seem larger. Exaggeration has always been the special danger of the "gifted" people (especially perhaps of evangelists). But it is at its deepest level dissatisfaction with God. Love rests in God and is satisfied. Love knows that God always does what is necessary and there is no need to blow it up in any way. Love does not puff up.

(d) *Love does not act unbecomingly*

The fourth danger is rudeness and disorderliness. Certain forms of order were being disregarded in Corinth: the women were becoming negligent concerning dress, the Lord's Supper was being misused, and at meetings for worship many took part in a disorderly manner. Because of this Paul admonishes them in 1 Corinthians 14:40, "All things should be done decently and in order."[2] It is important that people today who exercise these spiritual gifts (every born again Christian can be in this category!) should not neglect their dress and their use of time, in their work and in their private life. Where love is the highest law the person who exercises gifts will subject himself to God's authority, and to those to whom God has entrusted authority. He will not separate himself from the body of Christ, but in all humility will fulfill his ministry in the place where God has appointed him.[3]

(e) *Love does not seek its own*

As a summary of these four dangers Paul writes, "Love does not seek its own." Selfishness is the opposite of love. It is possible to seek for personal satisfaction in the exercise of spiritual gifts. It is possible for a Christian to feel insignificant and unwanted. But suddenly he discovers that he has a unique function in the body of Christ, and that his contribution to the body is necessary and important. He suddenly appears to be important in his own eyes and begins to seek personal gratification in the exercise of his charisma.

However, the opposite of selfishness is not the despising of oneself, but love—the love that seeks to please others. Actually it is only the person who does not despise himself, who can love. In order to love my neighbor, I must first learn to love myself. I can only love the other as much as I love myself. Jesus knew this when he said, "You must love your neighbor as yourself." To love oneself means that one accepts oneself as God created one; one says yes to one's gifts, one's position, one's vocation, one's opportunities, one's health, etc. Those who have not said yes to themselves and meant it, begin to seek more for themselves — which is true selfishness. Whoever lives in love says yes to himself and so to his neighbor. Love does not seek its own.

(2) *The Trial experienced by the Christian because of the Darkness in others.*

"Love is not provoked, it does not take into account wrong suffered, it does not rejoice at wrong; but love rejoices in the right." Verses 5b-6.

Not only are we not angels, but neither are our fellow Christians! Our fellow Christians also create burdens for us that become a trial to us.

(a) *Love is not provoked*

Our fellow Christians sometimes get on our nerves and irritate us. It is no wonder that we become irritable. We become a little harsh when we speak about them or to them. We cannot avoid the fact that there are people with whom we find it difficult to get on and who get on our nerves. It would be a form of pious deception if we tried to deny this fact. But we can avoid reacting harshly to them. It is not always easy, and it is quite possible that we have no psychological aptitude for it. L. Christenson once told the following example: "I know a man who worked with a woman who had a whole arsenal of annoying characteristics. He exercised all the will-power he had, to remain patient, to love her, understand her, and treat her kindly. But all that he produced was an artificial politeness. One morning he prayed in despair: 'Lord, I can't stand this woman. If you want her to receive love from me, then you will have to do it through me.' And from that moment on his thoughts, words and deeds were filled with a new power that began to influence the woman in an astounding way. Things went so far that people began to ask what had come over the woman."[4] If we cannot produce any love, then we ought at least to give Christ a chance to love the other person through us (it is, after all, His concern that the other is loved!). Love is not provoked.

(b) *Love does not take into account wrong suffered*

We encounter evil and wrong not only in ourselves but also in our brother. Humanly speaking it is understandable that we then begin to make lists and reckon up how often we have been treated badly. Certainly we are prepared to forgive if the other requests it, but hardly to the point where we also forget. But love keeps no lists, not even in the mind. Love forgets when it forgives. Forgiving without forgetting is not real forgiving, it is hypocrisy. Love begins afresh with every new encounter on the assumption that the other's approach is sincere (even if one has already been disappointed a hundred times — love has already forgotten them). Our neighbor can also begin to breathe more freely if we bring this kind of trust to the relationship. This trust brings new power to birth in him. (I am also a neighbor to others and therefore dependent on the fact that they do not hold the evil I have done against me.) Love has no use for a list of the other's misdeeds, for "love does not take into account wrong suffered."

(c) *Love does not rejoice at wrong*

To rejoice at our brother's wrong is natural. For then we are seen in a better light. Something is possibly confirmed that we "always knew" to be true. Some opponents of spiritual gifts lie in wait to find a person exercising gifts and behaving like a "traditional Pentecostal", so that their prejudice can be confirmed. Naturally the opposite danger also exists, that some who feel they are the "gifted" ones, rejoice when their opponents fall into slander and lovelessness, etc. Think of how many discussions in Christian circles would lose their fuel, if gossip and back-chat were excluded, and if love became the first law — love that does not rejoice at wrong.

(d) *Love rejoices in the right*

As a summary of this section on the darkness in others, Paul makes a positive statement: "Love rejoices in the right". Whoever is not irritated by others, forgets the evil done to him and does not rejoice in the wrongs of others, will find that his perception of the truth is sharpened. Not only the darkness in the neighbor becomes visible, but also the light. There are areas in one's brother's life through which the truth begins to shine — and love rejoices in this. This not only strengthens the light in one's brother, but also gives one the strength to call unrighteousness by its name when it arises. Only when I am rejoicing in the truth can I pull the beam out of my own eye and the mote out of my brother's.

(3) *The Trial experienced by the Christian because of the Darkness in God.*

"Love bears all things, believes all things, hopes all things, endures all things." Verse 7.

There are not only things that come between us and our neighbor, but also between us and God — things besides sin.

(a) *Love bears all things*

There are burdens that God lays on us that are not easy to

bear — burdens that we resent. Love bears all things! The Greek word for bearing means literally "protecting" and "enduring" or even "sacrificing". That is, love sacrifices the right to rebel against God. It will say: "How can God allow something like that?", but will bear it. Love protects God from those who would accuse Him, as for example Job's words when his wife began to accuse God: "Shall we receive good at the hand of God, and shall we not receive evil?" Love bears all things.

(b) *Love believes all things*

God is sometimes hidden. It seems as if He is not there. Every Christian, if he is honest, is subject at times to doubt. There are also times in the life of a Christian when he asks himself: "Isn't it all a matter of self-deception?" Love continues to believe even in such circumstances. It trusts, it remains true. Even the person who exercises spiritual gifts is subject to doubt. Not all people on whom he lays hands and prays recover. Not all the prophecies are fulfilled. Not all prayers are answered in the way he thought (despite deep and intense faith). Love believes despite all this. It penetrates through to the other side despite the mountains of doubt. It believes all things.

(c) *Love hopes all things*

God is sometimes veiled in darkness; but even then He is not out of reach, for we know with certainty that He is there. But He is there as a stranger, shrouded in mystery. He is the God who overcame Jacob at the brook Jabbok (Gen 32:22f). He is there as the God who drove Jesus into the wilderness to be tempted of the Devil (Mark 1:12). It is contrary to our dogmas that God should appear to us as the Stranger, the dark

One. Jakob Böhme had to suffer a great deal at the hands of his theological contemporaries for daring to defend this biblical truth. Whoever believes he has to understand God and justify Him in everything He does, has not yet truly encountered God. Love knows, "Even in hell thou art there," and because of this, hopes on. Hope is not a weak matter of considering something possible, but a strong knowledge in the sense of Romans 8:28, "We know that in everything God works for good with those who love him." Love hopes all things.

(d) *Love endures all things*

As a summary of his statements about the "darkness" of God, Paul writes, "Love endures all things." In placing burdens on us, in appearing hidden and dark at times, God is working on us, trying to chisel out the image of Christ in us and in the church. Paul writes in Colossians 1:24, "In my flesh I complete what is lacking in Christ's afflictions." There is nothing lacking in the actual suffering of Christ, but there is still something lacking in the suffering of Christ in the flesh of Paul. God chisels the image of Christ out of us, His raw material, through suffering and darkness. Oswald Chambers writes: "God's batterings always come in commonplace ways and through commonplace people."[5] We therefore cannot make too much of the sufferings of Christ within us; no one would understand us. We cannot brag about them; we can only endure them by not rising up against them. But there is nothing in *us* that can endure, only love can. The fourfold "all things" in verse 7 makes it quite clear that human possibilities are not under discussion here. In the last essence this verse talks about Jesus, "the pattern of all Christian existence" (Karl Barth).[6]

But just as Christ is the image of God (Col 1:15), so we are the image of Christ (Rom 8:29) i.e., Christ wants to become visible in our lives. Where love is present, Christ becomes manifest. Where Christ is visible, there is love. It is, consequently, not a matter of becoming over-active, or trying to produce love, but a matter of acknowledging our poverty and lack of love and thereby giving Christ the possibility of shining and working through us.

Love is Absolute—the Gifts Relative
(1 Cor 13 : 8-13)

"Love never ends; as for prophecy, it will pass away; as for tongues, they will cease; as for knowledge, it will pass away. For our knowledge is imperfect and our prophecy is imperfect; but when the perfect comes, the imperfect will pass away." Verses 8-10.

The gifts are necessary equipment for the pilgrim people of God. It is through the gifts (i.e., functions of the members of the body of Christ) that the church fulfils its responsibility in the world.[1] For every aspect of the total service of the Christian church there are appropriate spiritual gifts. G. Friedrich[2] classifies the gifts named in the New Testament as follows:

(a) Gifts of proclamation (Rom 12:6,7,8; 1 Cor 1:5f; 12:8, 10, 28; 13:2,8; Eph 4:11).

(b) Gifts of helping (Rom 12:7 [cf. Phil 1:1]; 12:8; 1 Cor 12:28; 13:3).

(c) Gifts of church leadership (Acts 20:28; Rom 12:8; 1 Cor 12:28; Eph 4:11 [cf 1 Pet 5:2f]; 1 Thess 5:12; 1 Tim 3:1; 5:17).

(d) Gifts of special powers (1 Cor 12:9, 10,28,30; 13:2).

(e) Gifts of prayer (1 Cor 12:10,28; 14:15-17).

It is not until our pilgrimage comes to an end that the spiritual gifts will cease.

Whoever teaches that they cease before then, is irresponsibly anticipating the end (*telos*).[3]

(a) *That which Continues*

"Love never ends."

According to verse 8, in contrast to everything temporary which decays and passes away, there is something that continues on and remains; love. Love belongs already to the coming world and consequently does not have to undergo any metamorphosis. Every Christian act, clothed in love, already anticipates in that which continues.

(b) *That which is Relative*

Prophetic utterances—will pass away.

Speaking in new languages—will cease.

Words of knowledge—will pass away.

The fact that the gifts will cease, does not mean that they are destroyed. In verse 12 it says expressly that there will be knowledge in the next world. Karl Barth quotes Blumhardt in this connection: "The Saviour is not a destroyer".[4] The gifts will be superfluous when that which is perfect has come. Prophecy will be replaced by a direct entry into the divine will and His secrets.

Speaking in other languages will become superfluous because what was "exceptional" shall become "normal".[5] We shall join in the choir of the heavenly hosts.

Words of knowledge will be superfluous when we see God face to face, when we participate directly in His unlimited wisdom.

Here on this earth the gifts are imperfect. They are limited by our body, our language, our comprehension, etc. In the gifts we grasp divine reality—but only imperfectly. When Christ returns the perfect will appear and the imperfect will cease.

Then we will see in all completeness that which previously was only partial.

(c) *Two helpful Images*

"When I was a child, I spoke like a child, I thought like a child, I reasoned like a child; when I became a man, I gave up childish ways. For now we see in a mirror dimly, but then face to face. Now I know in part; then I shall understand fully, even as I have been fully understood. So faith, hope, love abide, these three; but the greatest of these is love." Verses 11–13.

In the first image temporal and eternal realities are compared to childhood and maturity. A man does not think like a child and yet the thinking of a child is a preparatory stage on the way towards maturity. A man does not speak like a child and yet the babbling of a child is the beginning of true speech. "It is a matter of the thinking and speaking which are appropriate to the child and do not disqualify it as such."[6] In the second image (verse 12) that which is imperfect (the divine reality reflected in the gifts) is compared to an ancient metallic mirror which only gives an unclear and blurred representation. It does not present reality, only a reflection in reverse, which sometimes remains an enigma. This image reminds one of Plato's well-known parable of the cave.[7] In this parable the prisoners in the cave also see only a reflection of reality. But although the reflection is imperfect one has begun to see, and hopes to see more. Already in this life there is knowledge, and it will be there in the next life as well. The contrast is tremendous, but something of the original is contained in the reflection, and whoever sees the reflection receives intimations of the reality causing the reflection. The picture we see is a reflection of the other world in ours. "The gifts of the Spirit are signs of the presence of the coming Lord. They cease with the return of Christ."[8] In verse 13 (A.V.) Paul draws his discussion together by linking "and *now* abide . . ." (*nuni*) with the "*now* I know in part . . ." (*arti*) of verse 12. Paul says: *now,* in this age, faith, hope and love remain. W. Meyer says: "Faith is the outstretched hand with which we take hold of the grace of God. Hope is the holy perseverance with which we keep a firm hold on the grace of God. Love is the grace itself."[9]

Love is the greatest of the three, for love is not only for the "now" but for all eternity—even after faith has become sight and hope become fulfilment. Love still remains as love. Love is already the fulfilment and therein lies its unsurpassable greatness.

PART III

CHAPTER FOURTEEN

II

The Gift of Speaking in other Languages

In chapter 14 Paul is concerned above all with two questions:
(a) The relationship between speaking in other languages and
prophecy (verses 1–25), and (b) order in the meeting for
worship (verses 26–40).

In order to grasp more clearly the subject matter of this
chapter, in our exegesis we will examine each individual theme
separately (speaking in other languages — prophecy — the
meeting for worship). First of all, then, the matter of speaking
in other languages.

The Greek word *glossolalia* (*en glossais lalein* in the New
Testament) is usually translated "speaking in tongues". This
translation is unfortunate, for it breeds misunderstanding from
the outset. In English (and German), the word "tongue"
(*Zunge*) is used almost exclusively of the speech organ and only
seldom of a "language". In the Greek language today *glossa*
is still used of both "language" and "tongue" (the same is
true in the French *langue*). In his commentary on 1 Corinthians, Werner Meyer writes[1]: "Glossolalia is speaking in
languages. Certainly not, as is so often mistakenly assumed,
an inarticulate babbling and rolling of the tongue. The
tongue plays no other role in glossolalia than it does in normal
speech. The Greek word *glossa* carries the force here exclusively
of 'language'."

Following this linguistic explanation let us deal with the
statements of Paul in 1 Corinthians 14.

(a) *Positive Statements*

The first positive statement regarding speaking in other languages, has been made by Paul already in 12:28 when he says: "God has appointed . . . various kinds of languages." L. Christenson writes concerning this matter[2]: "Even if this were the only passage that mentions speaking in tongues, we would have to conclude that it is of abiding value, because *God* has ordained it so. Certainly God does not ordain anything for his church that is worthless, harmful, stupid, mad, or unimportant." There is the expression in 12:8,10 as well: "To one is given through the *Spirit* the utterance of wisdom . . . to another various kinds of languages." The Holy Spirit is also the author of speaking in tongues, as it says expressly in 12:11, "All these are inspired by one and the same Spirit." According to its origin then, tongues is a *charisma*, a gift from God.

A second positive statement is in 14:2 "For one who speaks in a tongue speaks not to men but to God." And what is he saying? " . . . he utters mysteries in the Spirit" (v.2). "For if I pray in a tongue, my spirit prays" (14:14). Paul maintains that the Spirit dwelling in man speaks to God in a way that is incomprehensible to man. But because the Spirit dwells in us and infuses our whole being, our total person is caught up in this praying, which is more direct and total than prayer with the mind. Paul expresses this in Romans 8:26f as follows: "For we do not know how to pray as we ought, but the Spirit himself intercedes for us with sighs too deep for words.[3] And he who searches the hearts of men knows what is the mind of the Spirit, because the Spirit intercedes for the saints according to the will of God." Besides this "prayer with the Spirit," prayer with the mind also has its rightful place. Paul says in 14:15 "I will pray with the spirit and I will pray with the mind also; I will sing with the spirit and I will sing with the mind also."

A third positive statement is found in 14:4 "He who speaks in a tongue edifies himself." The word "edification" may sound rather pious to us. This is not true of the original Greek word. What is meant is the constructive building up of the personality. Hollenweger characterizes this as the psycho-hygienic function of speaking in tongues.[4] He writes, "Man needs a non-intellectual means of meditation and release. Certain people find this release through art, others through speaking in tongues—and those who find release and balance through both fields are not as rare as was thought.[5]" Friedrich Heiler thinks, "that pouring out one's heart to God (Ps 42:4; 62:8) has the effect of an inner release that goes beyond the contribution of psychoanalysis."[6]

There is a group of psychoanalysts, especially from the school of C. J. Jung, who confirm the therapeutic effect of speaking in tongues. Morton Kelsey, theologian and psycho-therapist, writes: "There are people who without this experience would never have been able to come to psychological maturity. The experience of speaking in tongues opened them up to the unconscious and to a fuller, though more difficult life."[7]

At a conference of psychotherapists in New York in 1962, it was reported that a patient whose total "psyche" seemed to long for the experience of speaking in tongues, was influenced positively by the experience, despite the doubts and reservations of his doctor.[8] Dr. L. M. van Estveldt Vivier wrote a doctoral dissertation in speaking in tongues a few years ago for the Department of Psychiatry at the University of Johannesburg in South Africa. Through his research he was to establish whether a basic personality was the prerequisite for the appearance of glossolalia. Not only did Vivier discover that the Christians he examined were completely healthy and normal people, but also that they were better equipped to endure tension, i.e., to resist immediate gratification in lieu of more distant objectives.[9] A linguist with psychological training writes: "Speaking with tongues is one evidence of the Spirit of God working in the unconscious and bringing one to a new wholeness, a new integration of the total psyche, a process which the church has traditionally called sanctification."[10]

L. Christenson also gives examples of such growth in holiness and concludes: "When somebody prays in tongues he is built up in that area of his life and person which is in greatest spiritual need."[11] Because it is *God* who has appointed speaking in tongues, because it is the Holy Spirit who inspires tongues, because speaking in tongues increases the possibility of a deepened prayer life, and because speaking in tongues contributes towards the spiritual development of the personality, Paul can say in 14:18 "I thank God that I speak in tongues more than you all," and in 14:5 (literally) "I *desire* that you all speak in tongues." How dare Paul desire this? Only if it really is a *charisma* that is granted in principle to *all* Christians. L. Christenson assumes this when he writes [12]: "I am convinced that every Christian who desires this blessing, can ask God for it and receive it." Christenson then shows how this gift can be received.[13] Experience seems to prove that the majority of those who reach out simply to God, do receive the gift of speaking in another language. Psychologically the only explanation that satisfies me is the fact that this is a potential capacity, dormant in most people, awakened in the Christian by the Holy Spirit and filled with meaning. But what is the relationship of the desire of Paul "that you *all* speak in tongues" to his question in 12:30, "Do all speak with tongues?" All the commentaries are silent on this problem. "How can the contradiction with 12:30 be resolved?" asks Lietzmann hopelessly. L. Christenson suggests an answer to this dilemma; namely, that the statement in 12:30 has to do with the *public* manifestation of tongues—where naturally not all (14:27 only two or three) exercise this gift. His actual words are: "Whereas God only calls certain people to speak in tongues in a meeting, every believer can be blessed and edified personally through the manifestation of this gift in his private devotions."[14] I am not altogether satisfied with this answer, but I must admit that I have nothing better to put in its place. This is an open question as far as I am concerned.

One thing, however, is certain, that everyone conscious of need in this area, i.e., desiring to grow in prayer, can be certain that God will meet this need. Having discussed the private use of speaking in other languages in a Christian's communion with God, Paul now says that there is also a place for this gift in the meeting for worship: "When you come together, each one has a hymn, a lesson, a revelation, a tongue, or an interpretation. Let all things be done for edification. If any speak in a tongue, let there be only two or at most three, and each in turn; and let one interpret." So speaking in tongues in the meeting for worship does edify the church—albeit only when it is interpreted.

The gift of tongues when interpreted is equal in value to prophecy in the building up of the church, "He who prophesies is greater than he who speaks in tongues, *unless someone interprets*, so that the church may be edified" (14:5). Therefore he who speaks in tongues ought also to pray for the gift of interpretation, "Therefore, he who speaks in a tongue should pray for the power to interpret" (14:13). Thus far, we have examined Paul's positive statements concerning the gift of praying in the Spirit. Now we turn to his critical comments.

(b) Critical Comments

It strikes one immediately that Paul's critical comments are directed against speaking in tongues in *public*, especially uninterpreted speaking in tongues, not against the use of tongues in private devotions. Paul's first critical comment is: speaking in tongues in church without interpretation is useless. "Now, brethren, if I come to you speaking in tongues, how shall I benefit you unless I bring you some revelation or knowledge of prophecy or teaching? If even lifeless instruments, such as the flute or harp, do not give distinct notes, how will anyone know what is played? And if the bugle gives an indistinct sound, who will get ready for battle? So with yourselves; if you in a tongue utter speech that is not intelligible, how will anyone know what is said? For you will be speaking into the air. There are doubtless many different languages in the world, and none is without meaning; but if I do not know the meaning of the language, I shall be a foreigner to the speaker and the speaker a foreigner to me" (1 Cor 14:6–11). Paul compares speaking in tongues here with musical instruments and with foreign languages. He is alluding thereby to the two-fold use of tongues: in song and in prayer. The language of bugle calls includes both, because its melody contains a distinct message, and sounds out a clear call in place of spoken words. The meaning behind this comparison is quite clear: if a piece of music is strange to me and quite unknown, I cannot begin to do much with it. Personally, I can only make sense out of a concert if I have previously heard or read an interpretation of the musical numbers in question. Otherwise the different sounds do not register any meaning. If a bugle sounds out a call that no one understands, then no one will know how to respond to the signal. During the war, as a fourteen year old boy, I was a bugler for the fire brigade. We had a special tune in case of a fire; when we played it the fire brigade assembled (we were not allowed to practise this signal next to an open window!). If, however, we played some other signal, nothing happened, for the brigade would not understand it. If God wants to say something to the congregation, it must be clear and understandable—the signal must be interpreted.

The comparison with a foreign language is obvious: those listening to speaking in tongues, which is speaking in a foreign language, cannot understand if they do not know the language in question—unless someone translates. Therefore Paul concludes: "If you, in a tongue, utter speech that is not intelligible, how will anyone know what is said? For you will be speaking into the air" (14:9). Paul's second critical comment is: Uninterpreted speaking in tongues does not edify the listener: "Otherwise, if you bless with the spirit, how can anyone in the position of an outsider say the 'Amen' to your thanksgiving when he does not know what you are saying? For you may give thanks well enough, but the other man is not edified" (14:16,17). 14:23 also applies here: "If, therefore, the whole church assembles and all speak in tongues, and outsiders or unbelievers enter, will they not say that you are mad?"

The Greek word *idiotes* ("uninitiated" or "uninstructed") can refer to a baptismal candidate: but here it refers to a Christian not familiar with speaking in tongues, i.e., who has not been given the gift of interpretation (in other words, the one for whom the message is not interpreted). In Paul's opinion, neither the Christian nor the unbeliever is edified through speaking in tongues in church without interpretation. The unbeliever does not come through to faith and the

Christian cannot join in the prayer. From this, Paul concludes: "In church I would rather speak five words with my mind, in order to instruct others, than ten thousand words in a tongue" (14:19). And finally a third critical comment, 14:27, 28: "If any speak in a tongue, let there only be two or at most three, and each in turn; and let one interpret. But if there is no one to interpret, let each of them keep silence in church and speak to himself and to God." In the meeting of worship, therefore, not too many are to speak in tongues, only one at a time, and not without interpretation.

These are the three critical comments that Paul makes about tongues in congregational worship. With this criticism Paul is certainly not attacking this gift or minimizing it. To avoid being misunderstood along this line he says expressly at the end of his discussion of spiritual gifts: "Do not forbid speaking in tongues" (14:39).

The Gift of Prophecy

(a) *Positive Statements*

What applied to the gift of tongues also applies to prophecy: it is a gift of God's grace, inspired in the Christian by the Holy Spirit (1 Cor 12:10,11,28). Paul places a high value on this gift and praises it in a variety of ways. The first positive statement is in 14:3,4: "He who prophesies speaks to men for their upbuilding and encouragement and consolation . . . he who prophesies edifies the church." The edification of individual Christians and the whole congregation is the special task of prophecy.

The effect of prophecy is described as three-fold. We will look at each in turn. The Greek word *oikodome* (edification) is derived from *oikos* (house) and *domeo* (to build) and means literally "the building of a house". God Himself is the owner of the building (1 Cor 3:9, "you are . . . God's building"). Paul is the architect (literally in 1 Cor 3:10). In Corinth it was Paul who laid the foundation. Others (stone-mason, so-to-speak) built on this foundation. According to 1 Corinthians 3:12 these masons can add to the structure using a variety of materials ("gold, silver, precious stones, wood, hay, stubble"). The inferior materials will not stand the test (1 Cor 3:15, they will be consumed by fire)—and consequently do not contribute to edification. When Paul says that prophecy edifies the individual Christian and the church, he means that prophetic utterances belong to the good materials (as does the interpretation of tongues, 14:5b;) which are to be used in the building up of the church.

The second expression that Paul uses along with "edification" is *paraklesis*, in English "comfort". The verb *para-kaleo* from which this substantive is derived, means "to call someone", usually to give help (e.g., a defendant or someone to represent one before the law). When someone is "called alongside" and gives a helping hand, that means comfort and real spiritual help.

John characterizes the Holy Spirit Himself as this Comforter and Counsellor (John 14:16 *et al.*). In Romans 12:8 Paul lists this spiritual counselling and help among the gifts. (Besides "calling alongside", the word *para-kaleo* also means to encourage and exhort. Through encouragement and counsel the hearer is stimulated to direct action).

When Paul says that prophetic utterances serve to challenge the church he has a two-fold effect in mind:

(i) The Holy Spirit Himself coming amongst the members of the congregation as a comforter and giving spiritual counsel and help;

(ii) He also encourages the church to be obedient to the truth revealed through prophecy.

The third expression, *paramythia* (consolation), is closely related to the second. It can also mean counsel and comfort. Linguistically the word is derived from *para-mytheomai*. This verb (literally "to address") means to calm and pacify. Consolation, humanly speaking, does a person good. It calms the storms of fear, anxiety and despair. It helps us to rest in the presence of Jesus. That prophecy can work *para-mythia* is one of its best functions. It leads us away from the hectic bustle of daily affairs, away from the restlessness of this life, into the great peace of God.

A second positive statement appears in 14:24,25 "But if all prophesy, and an unbeliever or outsider enters, he is convicted by all, he is called to account by all, the secrets of his heart are disclosed; and so, falling on his face, he will worship God and declare that God is really among you."

In the gifts, the exalted Christ Himself is acting. Where Christ is at work things happen. Believers are edified, and unbelievers are confronted with the reality of God, so that they can find their way through to faith.

Paul lists a three-fold effect that prophecy has on the unbeliever (parallel to the three-fold effect on the believer):

the unbeliever is convicted,

the unbeliever is judged,

the unbeliever worships God.

We will look at this three-fold activity somewhat closer.

Above all, the unbeliever is convicted. The root (*legch*) of the Greek word *elegcho* means "to pounce on, attack, harm". From this has developed the more usual meaning "to curse, shame, overpower". According to Paul's presentation, prophecy immediately detects the sensitive spots (it "pounces" on them) and convicts, and thereby shames the sinner. That the Holy Spirit reveals what was secret is also supported in other places in the New Testament, e.g. John 2:25; 6:64; 13:11; 16:19; Acts 5:3; 1 Corinthians 2:11,15; 1 John 2:21. The convicting process consists in the fact that "the secrets of his heart are disclosed" (14:25). The "convicted" sinner is then judged by all. Paul uses the same word (*anakrinomai*) in 1 Corinthians 2:15 when he writes "the spiritual man judges all things". What does this judging involve? In Acts 25:26 this word is used of Festus' verdict on Paul. In this case it is a preliminary judgment. The final verdict is in the hands of the Emperor in Rome. In the same way every human judgment—also that of the Christian exercising any gift—is a preliminary judgment.[1] God will pass the ultimate verdict at the final day of Judgment. The judgment of the prophet does give the convicted sinner the possibility of turning to God. In submitting to the preliminary judgment of the prophet he will avoid the future condemnation of God.

The third effect of prophetic utterance consists in the fact that the convicted and judged sinner is converted to God. Although Paul knows from his own experience that authoritative proclamation can also work hardening in the hearer (e.g., Acts 13:45; 14:19; 17:5; 28:25f etc), in verse 25 he emphasizes the positive effect of prophecy. In this way he makes it clear that the intention of God is always the conversion of the sinner. When a man hardens his heart the divine Word cannot fulfil its rightful function.

Because the gift of prophecy edifies the church and because unbelievers are led to faith in Christ through this gift, it is to be cherished above all the others: "Earnestly desire the spiritual gifts, especially that you may prophesy," and again, "I want you all to speak in tongues, but even more to prophesy" (14:5). In desiring that *all* prophesy, Paul must have believed that this gift, together with the gift of tongues, is potentially present in every Christian. Here also one should be so at the disposal of the Holy Spirit that He can fan this *charisma* into a living fire.

(b) Critical Comments

Alongside these positive statements Paul makes two critical comments about prophecy. First of all he cautions them by saying order must prevail while there is prophesying in the meeting for worship. "Let two or three prophets speak" (14:29). The Christians referred to here are obviously members who have the office of a prophet.[2] These "recognized" prophets are not to participate too often, and should be silent when another receives a revelation (in the form of prophecy, it is to be assumed). "If a revelation is made to another sitting by, let the first be silent" (14:30). "Normal" members, who receive the gift of prophecy, have the "right of way", so to speak, and any number can take part as long as they do so in turn: "For you can all prophesy one by one, so that all may learn and all be encouraged; and the spirits of prophets are subject to prophets" (14:31,32). This last verse suggests that the gift of prophecy was widely distributed and could be exercised by many. A final regulation that Paul lays down is that prophecy ought to be tested: "Let two or three prophets speak, and let the others weigh what is said" (14:29). Why must prophets be tested?

Ludwig Albrecht in his notes on the New Testament says: "In prophesying there is a working together of the Holy Spirit with the human spirit. Man is a tool of the Holy Spirit, but a rational, free, co-operating partner, and therefore also responsible."

Whereas an evil spirit binds the will and temporarily destroys the personality of the one who submits to it, it is not so when the Holy Spirit takes possession — freedom and individuality remain (1 Cor 14:52; 1 Thess 5:19-20). The wonderful yet mysterious thing about prophesying is that the Holy Spirit, in all His perfection, combines with the human spirit in all its imperfection. One consequence of this, in our era and due to our weakness, is the fact that our prophecy is imperfect ("in part," 1 Cor 13:9). It is also obvious that the value and purity of our prophecy is conditioned by the state of the human channel (cf Rom 12:6).

W. Meyer writes in a similar vein: "Without succumbing

to the temptation of trying to probe into the psychology of prophets, it is quite possible to say that foreign elements (from the vast realm of the subconscious) can find their way into prophetic utterance and cloud and distort it. One prophecy would be so similar to another as to be indistinguishable — and yet arise from a different spiritual source. In a case such as this, rational "testing" would not suffice. Genuine prophecy at times calls for submission — an unsanctified mind, even though theologically trained, would rebel against this.

Prophecy makes an appeal for the total commitment of the hearer to the inspired Word. A foreign element in the midst of an inspired prophecy can only be detected charismatically, as one of the hearers is enlightened from above. This too could be called a prophetic gift — a specialized form of the Gift to diagnose imperfect prophecy.

The two critical comments Paul makes concerning prophecy are, therefore,

(1) order must be maintained as the Gift is exercised, and
(2) prophecy must be tested.

That Paul in no way wants to restrain the prophetic Gift in making these critical comments, is made clear at the end of the discussion when he challenges the church once more in 14:39, "So, my brethren, earnestly desire to prophesy."

Order in the Meeting for Worship
(1 Cor 14 : 26-40)

Although in the preceding paragraphs repeated reference has been made to the following text, we would like to consider verses 26–40 once more as a whole. In this text we find the oldest description of a Christian meeting for worship:

"What then, brethren? When you come together, each one has a hymn, a lesson, a revelation, a tongue, or an interpretation. Let all things be done for edification. If any speak in a tongue, let there be only two or at most three, and each in turn; and let one interpret. But if there is no one to interpret, let each of them keep silence in church and speak to himself and to God. Let two or three prophets speak, and let the others weigh what is said. If a revelation is made to another sitting by, let the first be silent. For you can all prophesy one by one, so that all may learn and all be encouraged; and the spirits of prophets are subject to prophets. For God is not a God of confusion but of peace—as in all the churches of the saints. Or did the word of God originate with you, or are you the only ones it has reached?

"If any one thinks that he is a prophet, or spiritual, he should acknowledge that what I am writing to you is a command of the Lord. If anyone does not recognize this, he is not recognized. So, my brethren, earnestly desire to prophesy, and do not forbid speaking in tongues; but all things should be done decently and in order."*

* In this text verses 34, 35 have been omitted for the following reasons:

What strikes one first in this description is the fact of the *whole* church in Corinth being gathered at one place (14:26; cf. 23 "If, therefore, the whole church assembles"). It is because of this that Paul could address the whole church with *one* letter. This means that at the one meeting the different streams of theological opinion were represented (cf. 11:18; 3:3,4), and also those from different strata of society (11:21, 22). According to 14:23,24 there were also instances when unbelievers (*apistoi*) were present. It was at gatherings such as this that the Lord's Supper was celebrated (see 1 Cor 11). And meetings for worship were conducted as described in verses 26–40.[1]

We might ask three questions about this passage:

(a) What happens at such a meeting for worship?
(b) How are the individual gifts exercised?
(c) What purpose does such a meeting fulfil?

(a) *What happens at such a meeting for worship?*

The first thing to note is that *everybody* has something to contribute. It is not *one person* alone who is prepared but everyone who comes along is inwardly ready to give. What he gives, however, is not his own, but a gift of the Spirit, a *charisma*. Jesus Himself ministers to those present through the gifts of His Spirit. In our text a few of the gifts relevant to the meeting for worship are mentioned. Naturally this means that other gifts, as for example a word of wisdom or knowledge, might also arise—the list is not exhaustive. Some of the gifts

---

(1) in a number of manuscripts they do not appear at this place,

(2) they seem out of place in this context,

(3) they contradict Paul's statement in 11:5 cf. K. Heim, *Die Gemeinde des Auferstandenen*, Munich, 1949, p. 204f, also Gottfried Fitzer, *Das Weib schweige in der Gemeinde*, Theol. Exist. Heute, NF, No. 110, and Johannes Leipoldt, *Die Frau in der antiken Welt und im Christentum*, Leipzig 1954, p. 189f.

mentioned here we have already discussed in detail in the exegesis of 1 Corinthians 12:8–11. Now let us examine the others—the first three: hymns, teaching, revelation.

(i) Hymns

Besides *psalmos*, the expression used here, Paul also makes use of *hymnos* and *ode* (Eph 5:19; Col 3:16). In all three concepts the stress is on praise. These meetings for worship, therefore, were times of thanksgiving and joy in the Lord. According to Eduard Schweizer, confession of sin was absent in these early meetings for worship.[2] The participants were sure of their salvation and could give all their attention to the praise and worship of God. In 1 Corinthians 14:15 Paul distinguishes between two kinds of singing: "I will sing with the spirit and I will sing with the mind also." "Singing with the spirit" is the result of direct inspiration. The melody and the words are both inspired directly by the Holy Spirit.[3] It is thought by some that the *Te Deum laudamus* of Ambrose came into being in this way. During the night before Easter in AD 387, at the baptism of Augustine, Ambrose and Augustine sang alternate lines under the direct inspiration of the Holy Spirit. Ambrose, moved by the Holy Spirit began, and Augustine also under inspiration answered line for line.[4] Such inspiration is described in the German hymnbook in these words: "Thy Spirit lifts my heart on high to Thee, that I may sing celestial psalms to Thee." 1 Corinthians 14:16 makes it clear that "singing with the spirit" occurs normally in a language unknown to the listeners.[5]

Besides singing with the spirit, there is also a place in the meeting for worship, for singing with the mind, i.e., songs written beforehand (in all likelihood Old Testament psalms were also sung). We can assume that such songs were begun by someone and the congregation joined in.

We are familiar with the content of some of these early hymns, because they appear in the New Testament text at various points, e.g. Revelation 4:11:

> "Worthy art thou, our Lord and God,
>   to receive glory and honour and power,
>   for thou didst create all things,
>   and by thy will they existed and were created."

It is also assumed that Philippians 2:6–11 was an early Christian hymn:

> "Though he was in the form of God,
>   did not count equality with God
>   a thing to be grasped,
>
> But emptied himself
>   taking the form of a servant,
>   being born in the likeness of men.
>
> And being found in human form
>   he humbled himself
>   and became obedient unto death, even death on a cross.
>
> Therefore God has highly exalted him
>   and bestowed on him the name
>   which is above every name,
>
> That at the name of Jesus
>   every knee should bow,
>   in heaven and on earth and under the earth,
>
> And every tongue confess
>   that Jesus Christ is Lord,
>   to the glory of God the Father."

Singing must have been an integral part of early Christian worship, for Pliny the younger writing to Emperor Trajan about their worship, says "They sing hymns to Christ as to a god."[6]

(ii) *Teaching*

The New Testament stresses the fact that teaching inspired by the Holy Spirit is different from all human instruction. For instance in Matthew 7:28,29 Jesus is said to have taught as one with divine authority—not like the scribes. In Mark 1:27 there is the exclamation "a new teaching!" made by some when they saw Him casting out an evil spirit. In John 7:46 some said of Jesus "no man ever spoke like this man". In Acts 13:12 the proconsul, we are told, "was astonished at the teaching of the Lord," and in 1 Corinthians 2:4 Paul describes his own teaching as—"not in plausible words of wisdom, but in demonstration of the Spirit and power."

Teaching as *charisma* is the Spirit of God becoming visible, not just our own human wisdom manifesting itself. The content of this teaching includes the whole realm of dogmatics and ethics, in other words everything that pertains to Christian faith and practice. Such Spirit-inspired teaching is recorded in all the writings of the New Testament, particularly in the letters. Because teaching is a gift of the Spirit it cannot be contained in static dogmas, for it is given afresh for each new situation. The Spirit is dynamic and cannot be preserved, not even in text books of dogma and ethics.

(iii) *Revelation*

Apokalypsis, the word Paul uses here, means literally "unveiling". According to the New Testament the veil that hides the divine world, will be removed before the eyes of mankind on the day of the Lord (Rev 1:7; Phil 2:10,11, etc.).

In the meantime a "gifted" Christian is now and then given

a glimpse of the mysteries of God's domain, i.e., he receives a revelation.[7] As a rule, revelations of this kind come through a prophetic word; sometimes, however, in the form of a vision. The *charisma* of visions had been already foretold by the prophet Joel (2:28f). This promise was fulfilled in the outpouring of the Holy Spirit at Pentecost, according to Acts 2:16,17 — consequently Spirit-filled Christians will occasionally receive visions. Often the meaning of the vision is clear (cf. Acts 16:9 "Come over to Macedonia and help us"). If the vision is not understood (cf Rev 7:13, "Who are these, clothed in white robes, and whence have they come?"; Acts 10:17, "Peter was inwardly perplexed as to what the vision he had seen might mean") then the revelation needs to be interpreted. In the *Shepherd of Hermas*, an early Christian writing, it says that a revelation is incomplete without the interpretation.[8] In a meeting for worship, we can imagine that the Christian would describe the vision he had received and would then give the interpretation himself or expect someone else to.

The content of a revelation is related to the unveiling of heavenly reality or of the divine plan of salvation. So Paul could write in Galatians 1:12 "For I did not receive it (the Gospel) from man, nor was I taught it, but it came through a revelation of Jesus Christ," or in Ephesians 3:3,6 "The mystery was made known to me by revelation . . . how the Gentiles are fellow heirs, members of the same body, and partakers of the promise in Christ Jesus through the gospel" (cf also Acts 22:17f; Acts 10:9f). Paul desires that Christian readers of this letter in like manner be given the "spirit of revelation" in order to know what are the "riches of his glorious inheritance" (Eph 1:17f).

Often clear guidance is given through visions.[9] As for example in:

Galatians 2:2	Paul is sent to Jerusalem,
Acts 9:10f	Ananias is sent to Paul,
Acts 10:3f	Cornelius is sent to Peter,
Acts 16:9f	Paul is called to Macedonia,
Acts 18:9f	Paul is told he must endure in Corinth,
Acts 22:17f	Paul receives the commission to go to the Gentiles.

Visions are also given as comfort and consolation to the church (e.g. Acts 27:23f, and especially the whole book of Revelation—the church's great book of comfort). When a member receives an insight into the inner meaning of God's great plan of salvation, the whole church is instructed, guided, and comforted.

(b) *How are the individual gifts exercised?*

The first principle to be observed in the exercise of the gifts is, "All things should be done decently and in order" (1 Cor 14:40). The other regulations all proceed from this foundation: only two or three should speak in tongues, each followed by its interpretation, the same applies to the prophets, only two or three, each tested in turn. What concerns Paul is that the members speak in turn and not simultaneously (14:28,30). Paul derives this principle from the nature of God, who is "not a God of confusion, but of peace" (14:33). It is significant that Paul makes "peace" the opposite of confusion, not "order". Confusion is dynamic; one cannot organize it. Organized confusion would no longer be confusion; it would be order—of a bad variety. Static order is not in keeping with dynamic confusion, but dynamic peace is. A charismatic meeting for worship cannot be ordered and controlled by some wooden scheme or formula. Order results when all the members listen to the one Spirit and when each member regards the other as better than himself (Phil 2:3). Then the result is peace, dynamic orderliness. Confusion is not the normal state of affairs when the gifts are exercised—apparently Corinth was the exception. In no other letter were admonitions of this kind necessary, although we know that spiritual gifts were exercised in the other churches.[10] In Corinth there was not only confusion when the gifts of the Spirit were being exercised, but also during the Lord's Supper (1 Cor 11:20f) in matters of dress (1 Cor 11:13f), in moral questions (1 Cor 5:1f) etc. Order reigned in other congregations (1 Cor 11:16; 12:26; Col 2:5). In Thessalonica Paul had to admonish the members not to suppress the spiritual gifts (1 Thess 5:19,20). The regulations Paul introduces are only designed, therefore, to regulate the exercise of gifts and in no way to suppress them (1 Cor 14:39).

(c) *What is the purpose of such a meeting for worship?*

"Let all things be done for edification" (1 Cor 14:26). The church is the body of Christ. It is an organism; not an organization. Every organism has its laws of development. Each individual member grows (1 John 2:12f), as does also the total organism.

Besides "edifying oneself" (1 Cor 14:4) it will mean "building up one another". The individual is built up through the functioning of the other individual members of the body of Christ (cf. Rom 1:11; 14:19; 15:2), above all through the work of the apostle, who, according to 2 Corinthians 10:8 and 13:10, is given special authority to build up individual members and the total church. Paul is certainly conscious of this authority[11] when he writes in 1 Corinthians 14:37,38: "if anyone thinks that he is a prophet, or spiritual, he should acknowledge that what I am writing to you is a command of the Lord. If anyone does not recognize this, he is not recognized." The Spirit recognizes the Spirit (1 Cor 2:10f). If the individual members obey the commands of their Lord received through the apostles (this is what it means to confess Jesus as "Lord", see commentary on 12:3) they are edified. If they reject these commands, they are relinquishing their discipleship and will destroy themselves.

K. Heim writes: "To be recognized means: to be recognized by Christ in the Great Judgment."[12] Whoever does not recognize the command of the Lord in that of the apostle, is inviting upon himself the judgment of Jesus in Matthew 7:23 "I never knew you." But the edification of the total body is the primary concern, not just that of the individual. It is possible for a whole congregation to remain in the infant stage (1 Cor 3:1f). The gifts and ministries of the Spirit are given so that the *total* body can reach maturity in Christ, as Paul describes it in Ephesians 4:11–16.

"And his gifts were that some should be apostles, some prophets, some evangelists, some pastors and teachers, for the equipment of the saints, for the work of the ministry, for building up the body of Christ, until we all attain to the unity of the faith and of the knowledge of the Son of God, to mature manhood, to the measure of the stature of the fullness of Christ; so that we may no longer be children, tossed to and fro and carried about with every wind of doctrine, by the cunning of men, by their craftiness in deceitful wiles. Rather, speaking the truth in love, we are to grow up in every way into him who is the head, into Christ, from whom the whole body, joined and knit together by every joint with which it is supplied, when each part is working properly, makes bodily growth and upbuilds itself in love."

Notes

Chapter 1

[1] The Greek *pneumatikon* is the genitive of both the masculine and the neuter. It could also be translated "concerning those who exercise spiritual gifts".

[2] It is regrettable that instruction in the church today (with few exceptions) ends with confirmation. It is an urgent matter to see that *all* are instructed.

[3] Similar small bronze images, three inches high on the average, have been excavated in large numbers.

[4] There are still many ecstatic cults of this kind in pagan religions, cf. E. Dammann, *Die Religionen Afrikas*, Stuttgart, 1963, p.76f.

[5] That this expression occurred during the meetings for worship seems clear from the context. From chapter 11 onwards Paul is dealing with questions related to their gatherings.

[6] W. Schmithals, *Die Gnosis in Korinth*, 1956, p.47.

[7] Origen, *Contr. Cels.*, V, 1, 28.

[8] The Orthodox liturgy is still a reminder of this. Before the confession of faith, the cry arises, "The door, the door!" as a sign of the fact that the door has to be closed behind the non-Christians who had to leave.

Chapter 2

[1] Cf. E. Schweizer, *Die Gemeinde nach dem Neuen Testament*, Zurich, 1949, p.6.

[2] The expressions "gifts of divine grace" and "spiritual gifts" are synonymous. Spiritual gifts are concretizations of the divine Spirit, cf. E. Käsemann, *Essays on New Testament Themes*, London, 1964, p.63f.

[3] A list of the various gifts related in the New Testament to the word *charisma* appears in the appendix to my article, *Der frühchristliche Gottesdienst* (Oekum. Texte and Studien, Heft 30).

Chapter 4

[1] Joseph Brosch, *Charismen und Ämter in der Urkirche*, Bonn, 1951, p. 56f.

[2] Ibid, p. 50.

[3] Ibid, p. 51, note 131.

[4] Cf. also Zacharias in Luke 1:20.

[5] Cf. also Isaiah 53:4.

[6] Trust of this kind seems to be a prerequisite for healing, cf. Mark 6:5f; Matthew 13:58.

[7] Examples of the use of spittle in healing in the history of religions can be found in E. Klostermann, *Handbuch zum Neuen Testament*, Tübingen, 1919, Bd 11, p. 62.

[8] It is in Jesus' disciples as well that the sick person encounters Christ, even if indirectly, cf. Galatians 2:20; 1 Corinthians 4:16; Ephesians 5:1.

[9] H. Doebert, *Das Charisma der Krankenheilung*, Hamburg, 1960, p. 70f.

[10] J. Brosch, *op. cit.*, p. 57; cr. also Emil Brunner, *The Misunderstanding of the Church*, London, 1952, p. 57f.

[11] In his book, *Die Erlebnisechtheit der Apokalypse des Johannes*, Leipzig, 1930, Carl Schneider has shown that visions recorded in the Book of Revelation were genuine visions, not just a random arrangement of existing apocalyptic images.

[12] Cf. A. Bittlinger, *Der frühchristliche Gottesdienst*, p. 18.

[13] In Acts 5 the discernment of spirits is linked with prophecy, see 1 Corinthians 14:24.

[14] In quoting Isaiah in 1 Corinthians 14:21, Paul is saying that when "prayer with the spirit" is misused, it resembles worthless ecstatic gibberish, which has no place in a meeting for worship. Is it not a judgment upon the church when it is addressed in the same way as the Assyrians addressed apostate Israel?

[15] In contrast to zawlazaw - kawlakaw, we are dealing here with a true language.

[16] We are dealing here with a prayer, cf. Vincent Taylor, *The Gospel according to St. Mark*, London, 1959, p. 355: "The use of *anablepo* 'to look up' here and in Mark 6:41 indicates the act of prayer."

[17] R. Bultmann, *The History of the Synoptic Tradition*, Oxford, 1963, pp. 213, 137, 147.

[18] For example see R. Bultmann, *op. cit.*, pp. 222–23. The word in Mark 7:34 is probably Aramaic (for derivatives see Klostermann). It is remarkable, however, that Mark includes such words only at 5:41 and 7:34, and not at other places, such as 4:39. Possibly Mark is implying that Jesus spoke differently in 5:41 from how He normally spoke.

[19] Kurt Kuhl, *The Prophets of Israel*, Edinburgh 1960.

Chapter 6

[1] Vincent Taylor, *op. cit.*, p. 626f.

[2] Ibid, p. 627.

[3] Ralf Luther, *Neutestamentl. Wörterbuch*, 7. Ed., p. 11f.

[4] John Calvin, *Institutes*, IV/3/4.

[5] E. Schweizer, *Church Order in the New Testament*, London, 1961, p. 197.

[6] Paul Tillich, *The Shaking of the Foundations*, London, 1962, p. 17.

[7] Siegfried Bucholz, *Nachahmung des Menschen*, Wuppertal, 1968.

[8] W. Hollenweger, *Der 1 Korintherbrief, eine Arbeitshilfe zur Bibelwoche*, 1964–65, p. 25f.

Chapter 7

[1] Gerhard Iber, *Zum Verständnis von 1. Korinther* 12, 31, ZNW, 1963, p. 43f.

[2] Ibid, p. 49.

[3] Ibid, p. 52.

[4] In discussion W. Becker discerned rightly that love is *the* fruit of the Spirit. Galatians 5 ought then to read: the fruit of the Spirit is love, i.e., love as joy, love as peace, love as patience, etc.

[5] Cf. L. Christenson, *Die Bedeutung der Gnadengaben für die Gemeinde Jesu Christi*, 1964, p. 90f.

[6] Cf. W. Meyer, *Der 1. Brief an die Korinther*, 1945, Vol II, p. 160f.

[7] The various functions of the body of Christ in L. Christenson, *Die Bedeutung der Gnadengaben*, p. 90.

[8] E. Käsemann. *op. cit.*, p. 83.

Chapter 8

[1] W. Meyer, *op. cit.*, p. 163f.

[2] W. Hollenweger, *op. cit.*, p. 29.

Chapter 9

[1] In sectioning verses 4–7 I am following Karl Barth, *Church Dogmatics* IV/2, Edinburgh, 1958, p. 831f. The reader may notice that I am indebted to Karl Barth in my whole discussion of 1 Corinthians 13.

[2] Cf. A. Bittlinger, *Der frühchristliche Gottesdienst*, p. 20f.

[3] Cf. 1 Corinthians 3:5f; Galatians 2:1f, see also Plato's *Dialog on Criton*.

[4] L. Christenson, *Die Bedeutung der Gnadengaben*, p. 113.

[5] Oswald Chambers, *My Utmost for His Highest*, London, 1963, p. 278.

[6] Karl Barth, *op. cit.*, p. 835.

Chapter 10

[1] Cf. the commentary on 1 Corinthians 12:12f.

[2] G. Friedrich, *Geist und Amt*, in *Wort und Dienst, neue Folge*, 3 Bd, 1952, p. 83f.

[3] W. Hollenweger, *op. cit.* p. 30.

[4] K. Barth, *op. cit.*, p. 837.

[5] Ibid, p. 837.

[6] Ibid, p. 839.

[7] Plato, *Staat*, p. 514f.

[8] Rheinland-Theses on the theme *Church and Charisma* 11. 2.h. printed in A. Bittlinger, *Der frühchristliche Gottesdienst*, p. 32.

[9] W. Meyer, *op. cit.*, p. 186.

Chapter 11

[1] W. Meyer, *op. cit.*, vol 11, p. 194, cf. on the whole question of speaking in tongues A. Bittlinger, *Das Sprachenreden in der Kirche, seine Bedeutung und Problematik in Vergangenheit und Gegenwart*, Hanover, 1965.

[2] L. Christenson, *Die Bedeutung der Gnadengaben*, p. 73.

[3] Concerning the Greek expression *stenazo* ("sighing") as an official expression for prayer other than with the mind, see Carl Schneider, *Geistesgeschichte des antiken Christentums*, Vol I, p. 224f. Similar conclusions arrived at, among others, by Th. Zahn, 1925, p. 413; H. Lietzmann, 1910, p. 45; O. Michel, 1955, p. 178. in their commentaries on Paul's letter to the Romans.

[4] W. Hollenweger, *op. cit.*, p. 26.

[5] Ibid, p. 27.

[6] F. Heiler, *Ecclesia Caritatis*, 1965, p. 164.

[7] Morton J. Kelsey, *Speaking with Tongues*, London, 1965.

[8] Ibid, p. 200.

[9] Ibid, p. 204f.

[10] Ibid, p. 222.

[11] L. Christenson, *Die Bedeutung der Gnadengaben*, p. 78.

[12] L. Christenson, *Speaking in Tongues, a gift for the Body of Christ*, London, 1963, p. 19.

[13] Ibid, p. 20f.

[14] Ibid, p. 19.

Chapter 12

[1] Cf. L. Morris, *The First Epistle of Paul to the Corinthians*, London, 1958, p. 60. In classical Greek the verb *anakrinomai* always carries the meaning of a preliminary judgment (cf. Bruce, *The Acts of the Apostles*, p. 120).

[2] Cf. commentary on 1 Corinthians 12:28. The difference between the gift of prophecy and the office of a prophet consists in the fact that the one who possesses the office receives an enduring commission (cf. the Old

Testament prophets who were called specially by God), whereas the gift of prophecy is only given now and then to any of the Spirit-filled church members.

Chapter 13

[1] Meetings for worship as described in 1 Corinthians 14 were not only conducted in Corinth, but also in a similar way in other Pauline churches, and in the post-apostolic age (cf. E. Schweizer, *Worship in the Early Church*, London, p. 5f). The following are a few references to the exercise of spiritual gifts in the post-apostolic period: Irenaeus, V, 6; Justin, *Dial. Tryph.*, chapters 82,88; Origen, *Contr. Cels.*, 1:46; VII:8; *Acta Perpetua et Felicitatis*, chapter 7; Tertullian, *Contr. Marc.*, V:8; *De Anima* 9; Ign. Smyrna Intr.; 1 Clement 38:1.

[2] E. Schweizer, *Church Order in the New Testament*, p. 207.

[3] Martin Luther asserts in his *Tabletalks* that the Holy Spirit inspired the melody and text of *Komm Heiliger Geist, Herre Gott* (*Handbuch zum EKG*, Sonderband, p. 164, Göttingen, 1958).

[4] For the original text of this song and the legend about its origin, see *Handbuch zum EKG*, Sonderband, p. 220.

[5] Eduard Schweizer writes the following in a letter to the author (22.11.63): "1 Corinthians 14:15 seems to presuppose that singing in the Spirit is not understood by the congregation, for they cannot say 'Amen'."

[6] *Brief X*, 96; other early Christian hymns: John 1:1f; 1 Timothy 3:16; Luke 1; Ephesians 1; Colossians 1, etc.

[7] A. Oepke differentiates between an eschatological and mystical use of the word *apokalypsis* (Th WNT, Vol 3, p. 589).

[8] Vis. III, 10, 9.

[9] These visions were not given during a meeting for worship and are only relevant here in so far as they emphasize the frequency of visionary experiences. It is probable, however, that some visions, experienced outside of meetings, were shared with the church at worship.

[10] As for example in Ephesus (Acts 19:6); cf. also footnote 1.

[11] Cf. also 1 John 4:6.

[12] K. Heim, *op. cit.*, p. 206.